YOUR PERSONAL LIFE DIARY

USE ASTROLOGY TO PREDICT TIMES OF MAJOR CHANGES IN YOUR LIFE AND SOW, REAP, AND HARVEST YOUR OWN "CROP" WITHOUT A BIRTH CHART

By Brian. T. Baulsom M.N.F.S.H

B

ISBN 978-0-9930926-1-9

HOW TO USE THE BOOK

PROVE IT FOR YOURSELF

1. **FILL IN THE LIFE DIARY FORM WITH KNOWN PAST EVENTS.**
   (Please see downloads below). Look for the yellow highlights to see when main events occur. Note that opportunities for "new beginnings" occur at 12 and 30 year intervals.

2. **CONTINUE READING TO SEE HOW TO USE IT IN THE FUTURE.**

THE METHOD

1. Download the form or use the one on the next pages.

2. Fill in the years starting with the year of your birth.

3. Add notes against years when changes occurred in your life like :-

   - House moves
   - Partnership changes
   - Job changes
   - Health problems
   - Beginning and end of activities
   - Birth of children
   - Etc.

4. Read how you can use this information to align your actions with Universal Law to sow your own "seeds" and reap your own harvest.

Please note that Years run from birthday to birthday – so we need to take this into account. For example, with August to December birthdays, events are likely in the following years.

FREE DOWNLOADS

FREE LIFE DIARY FORM DOWNLOAD

The 2 page Life Diary Form is available in the following versions :-

- FILLABLE/PRINTABLE PDF
- FILLABLE/PRINTABLE EXCEL SPREADSHEET

FREE PDF PICTURE BOOK DOWNLOAD

This book is 80 pages of pictures extracted from my book "The Cycle of Growth" to be published in 2015 - which is A4 size to allow for better reproduction of the numerous tables and diagrams included – many of which are in colour.

PLEASE DOWNLOAD FROM HERE :- www.CycleOfGrowth.com

By leaving your email address you will be given notification of special offers on my books.

Page 1 : AGES 0 TO 41 **GENERIC HOUSES**

	Age	Year	Event	Ju	Sa	Ur
1	0		* * * BIRTH	1	1	1
2	1			2	1	1
3	2			3		
4	3			4		
5	4			5		
6	5			6		
7	6			7		
8	7			8	4	
9	8			9	4	2
10	9			10		
11	10			11		
12	11			12		
13	12		*	1		
14	13			2		
15	14			3		3
16	15			4	7	
17	16			5	7	
18	17			6		
19	18			7		
20	19			8		
21	20			9		
22	21			10		4
23	22			11	10	
24	23			12	10	
25	24		*	1		
26	25			2		
27	26			3		
28	27			4		
29	28			5		5
30	29			6		
31	30		*	7	1	
32	31			8	1	
33	32			9		
34	33			10		
35	34			11		
36	35			12		6
37	36		*	1		
38	37			2	4	
39	38			3	4	
40	39			4		
41	40			5		
42	41			6		

"Life Diary" by Brian Baulsom

Figure 1 : Life Diary Form - Page 1

Page 2 : AGES 42 TO 83 GENERIC HOUSES

	Age	Year	Event	Ju	Sa	Ur
43	42			7		7
44	43			8		
45	44			9		
46	45			10	7	
47	46			11	7	
48	47			12		
49	48		*	1		
50	49			2		8
51	50			3		
52	51			4		
53	52			5	10	
54	53			6	10	
55	54			7		
56	55			8		
57	56			9		9
58	57			10		
59	58			11		
60	59			12		
61	60		* *	1	1	
62	61			2	1	
63	62			3		
64	63			4		10
65	64			5		
66	65			6		
67	66			7		
68	67			8	4	
69	68			9	4	
70	69			10		
71	70			11		11
72	71			12		
73	72		*	1		
74	73			2		
75	74			3		
76	75			4	7	
77	76			5	7	
78	77			6		12
79	78			7		
80	79			8		
81	80			9		
82	81			10		
83	82			11	10	
84	83			12	10	

"Life diary" by Brian Baulsom

Figure 2 : Life Diary Form - Page 2

** SUMMARY TABLE OF CHAPTERS **

(Full Table Of Contents follows)

** TABLE OF CONTENTS **

** TABLE OF FIGURES **

* * * * * * * * * * * * * * * * * * * *

FAITH

IS CONTINUING TO DISCARD THE ABSURD

EVEN IN THE FACE OF THE UNKNOWN
[Anon]

* * * * * * * * * * * * * * * * * * * *

When you have eliminated the impossible,

whatever remains, however improbable,

must be the truth.

[Sir Arthur Conan Doyle- Sherlock Holmes]

* * * * * * * * * * * * * * * * * * * *

WE CAN APPLY THIS TO
THE CONCEPT OF REINCARNATION

INTRODUCTIONS

INTRODUCING THE BOOK

The book assumes that the reader has no knowledge of Astrology and therefore contains deliberate repetition to help understanding. This is in keeping with the principle of repetitive cycles.

Astrology was first used in agricultural communities as an annual "calendar" to sow and reap crops. We can use those same Universal Principles to sow seeds and reap other forms of "harvest".

This book is part of nearly 40 years of research and contains original concepts not found anywhere else. It began as part of another, much bigger, book called "The Cycle of Growth" which currently consists of 480 A4 pages, so will need to be split into 2 volumes (NB. This may change). "The Cycle of Growth" compares Astrology with other traditional esoteric subjects such as Psychology, Tarot, Numerology, and The Kabbalah which I have updated to include new scientific discoveries. It contains some amazing new discoveries of its own. There is a more detailed description at the end of this book.

One of the concepts I developed was the "Life Diary", which embodies the principles of Astrology and "The Cycle of Growth" whilst enabling a more practical application without the need for a Birth Chart.

Both books begin by assuming that the reader has little or no knowledge of any of the subjects, so more experienced astrologers can skip the early chapters of this one. They are not meant to be complete Astrology tutorials – the focus is on understanding that all cycles, no matter how many stages we split them into are all manifestations of the same Whole. This gives a broader overview than is achieved by traditional methods. Here we have a practical experiment.

The main chapters here are :-

1. HOUSES – which is the fixed basis of an Astrological Birth Chart.
2. ZODIAC SIGNS – which enable us to add Planet positions to Astrological charts.
3. TRANSITS – which examine the movement of Planets after birth.
4. EXAMPLE CHARTS – The Birth Chart and Transits of Lady Diana Spencer.
5. THE LIFE DIARY – how to examine Planet Transits in your life.
6. THE CYCLE OF GROWTH – information about the book and how to get Volume 2 free.

INTRODUCTIONS

INTRODUCING MYSELF

My middle name is Thomas. The reason I state that is because, in relation to this book, it seems to be as important as my first. In the Bible "Doubting Thomas" was the disciple of Jesus who refused to believe the resurrection had occurred until he had seen Jesus for himself, and touched his wounds. He did get the evidence he wanted. I too tend to disbelieve what people tell me and look for empiric proof, or tangible evidence, when considering important matters.

I had a fairly normal life without any knowledge or interest in "occult" subjects (occult, really, just means "hidden") until age 34 when I had some unusual experiences which led me, via Spiritualism, to discover an ability for healing and realise that there is more to life than what we perceive with our normal 5 senses. I have met people who, when I mention occult subjects, accuse me of "dabbling". I realise that I never dabble. Once I am interested in a subject I pursue it in some depth. This book covers over 30 years of study, practical experience, and experiment .

Although I eventually qualified as a full member of *The National Federation of Spiritual Healers* in the United Kingdom (now under the umbrella of *The Healing Trust*) and achieved probationer certificates with *The Institute of Spiritualist Mediums* as Spirit Communicator and Speaker I decided that these areas did not hold enough information about how things "worked", or, if there is a purpose to life, what it is. The same can be said about The Tarot. Having given hundreds of readings for people unknown to me, and being amazed at the accuracy, it was more interesting to put the cards back in order to see their overall story better.

My main interest is Astrology because not only does it have a scientific basis but is open to more scientific experimentation. It also gives a broader overview on life than the other disciplines which tend to be limited to more day-to-day mundane activities. This is mainly because of the requirements of the client at the time. I am more interested in events in the context of a whole lifetime than day to day events. It is for this reason that, even though I had begun to pursue the subjects on a professional basis, I decided to return to a "normal" job so that I could approach them in my own way, at my own speed.

INTRODUCTIONS

INTRODUCING ASTROLOGY

USE ASTROLOGY TO PREDICT TIMES OF MAJOR CHANGES IN YOUR LIFE AND USE THEM

Astrology as we know it today began in Mesopotamia at around 3000 BC with the recognition that certain star patterns were visible at sunrise at specific times of the year. As the sun continued to rise they became invisible. At that time the lifestyle was based on Agriculture, and there was a need for some kind of Calendar for the population to know when to sow and reap their crops. There were no cities, and no reading or writing among the general population.

The next step in development was to compare the star patterns in the heavens with what was happening on earth at the time and to give them names. It is quite easy to see how the sight of rams competing with one another at the beginning of Spring became associated with the picture of a ram in the sky.

From there we have the development of the 12 Signs of The Zodiac (Zodiac means "circle of animals") which became the first virtual calendar. "Virtual" because it was not written down. Everything was "controlled" by the Sun in the heavens.

From the recognition of the changing patterns there developed a need to know when the annual cycle ended and a new one began. We now understand that the first day of Spring begins at sunrise on the day of the Spring Equinox - when day and night are of equal length of 12 hours. In Astrological terms this defines the entry of the Sun into the Sign of Aries at Zero degrees. From there the 360 degree circle is divides into 12 equal portions of 30 degrees to designate the 12 Signs. How the ancients arrived at this conclusion in the absence of clocks can only be imagined. My suggestion is that this is one of the reasons for the building of Pyramids, Ziggurats, Henges, and other stone circles like Stonehenge which began at this time. We do know that they were arranged to show the sun's position on very specific days of the year. Their following decline is also explained by the later growth of reading and writing making them unnecessary.

All this began the "Age of Aries". Nowadays, having the benefit of written calendars and accurate clocks we have tended to discard The Zodiac Calendar. There is also the recognition that the Sun no longer rises in Aries on the morning of the Spring Equinox. This is due to "The Precession of the Equinoxes" caused by the earth wobbling on its axis like a top - so the axis has a cycle of its own which lasts 26,000 years. If we divide this cycle by 12 we get approximately 2,160 years for each Zodiac Sign. The rotation of the axis is in the opposite direction to the Zodiac Signs, so 3000 BC to 900 BC was the Age of Aries, 900 BC to 1200 AD the Age of Pisces, and we are now in The Age of Aquarius. All this is approximate. I make more accurate calculations in my book "The Cycle of Growth" using known historical events.

Opponents of Astrology suggest that this negates the practice of Astrology and makes it meaningless. However, we have the following facts :-

- Anyone who studies Astrology gets evidence that it does actually work. This book is a further opportunity to validate that fact.
- There is a general misunderstanding that the external Zodiac star patterns still apply to life on earth. As we have seen, what actually happened was that they were originally used to establish our annual calendar IN RELATION TO THE EARTH'S ANNUAL CYCLE AROUND THE SUN. From then on the Zodiac Circle became an imaginary EARTH CENTRED "annual clock" which is reset each year as already described. The principle is the same as that which establishes the imaginary lines of latitude and longitude used in navigation, and which also have zero points which were arbitrarily fixed at some time in the past.

- Zero degrees of Aries is still reset at the Spring Equinox, and is the beginning of the agricultural year on earth, as demonstrated by the activities of its plants and animals - who have no other choice. The relationship between Earth and the Sun has not changed.
- The Zodiac Signs are still used to accurately locate the positions of the planets for any time past, present, or future - in relationship to earth as a fixed point.

CONCLUSION

Study of the Zodiac Cycle of Growth has established that it applies to all creative activities - which have "seed", "growth", "harvest", and "death" times, as in the annual cycle of Nature. What has been missing until now is the recognition that we are affected by cycles other than the annual one. For example, we recognise a Spring, Summer, Autumn, and Winter of a human lifetime. Also, we are now no longer bound to the annual cycle of an agricultural life, and have the opportunity to use them. This book is an attempt to show how we can continue to use Astrology to uncover and work with those natural cycles in the same way, so we can sow and reap with less effort

THE COVER PICTURE COMPONENTS

Figure 3 : The cover picture components

Part 1 : THE CHRYSOPOEIA OF CLEOPATRA

The original "serpent" shows an endlessly repeating cycle - without development or evolution.

**The Ancient Greek words enclosed within the image of the 'Ouroboros' (Greek letters, ουροβόρος όφις meaning "tail-devouring snake") from "The Chrysopoeia of Cleopatra" ("Gold manufacture/'Gold-Making of Cleopatra, the alchemist) dating to ca. 2nd. century AD mean literally : "The one the all-seeing/ including", i.e. "One is All". ("hen to panops "in Latin transliteration; "έν τό πάνοψ" in Greek letters).*

[Ref <http://en.allexperts.com/q/Greek-2004/2008/12/Ouroboros.htm>]

Part 2 : TAROT CARD X.THE WHEEL OF FORTUNE

- The picture is of a wheel endlessly turning.

It has, among other things, relationships with :-

- The Earth
- All cycles of Nature and other Wheels as contained in The Cycle of Growth.
- The Vision of Ezekiel and The Book of Revelation.
- The board game "Snakes and Ladders" (up the ladders, back down the snakes)

Part 3 : "THE CYCLE OF GROWTH" .....

.... WHICH CONTAINS A "TRANSCENDENT OCTAVE" NOT COVERED HERE.

BIRTH CHART HOUSES

This chapter introduces the structure of Houses in a Birth Chart.

There are examples of Lady Diana Spencer's Birth Chart and Transit Chart in the chapter [CHARTS EXAMPLES].

In this book we are concerned with 2 types of Houses :-

1. **PERSONAL HOUSES** *refer to the 12 Houses that form the basic structure of a Birth Chart. At this level there is no variation. Without adding the details of Planets and Zodiac Signs we are all the same. This is the 98% of DNA that makes us human. A Birth Chart is a like a "map" showing the positions of Planets at the time of birth. The orientation of the House Wheel is calculated according to the birth time and place of an individual. This depends on the 24 hour rotation of The Earth and so requires an accurate birth time. We then use the Astrological Signs to add the Planets. The Personal Houses relate to our whole life from Conception (Cycle of Growth Stage 9) to Death (Cycle of Growth Stage 8).*

   PERSONAL HOUSES ARE DESCRIBED IN THIS CHAPTER

2. ***GENERIC HOUSES*** *refer to the individual Transit cycles of each separate Planet and did not form part of traditional Astrology.*

   GENERIC HOUSES ARE DEALT WITH IN THE CHAPTER [TRANSITS]

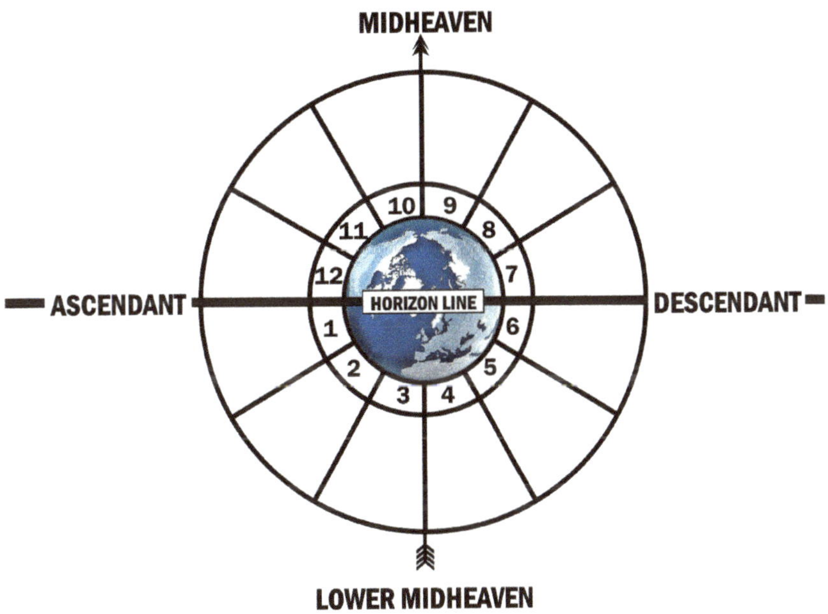

Figure 4 : The Personal House basis of an astrological chart

THE BIRTH CHART

Here we deal with how the Personal Houses are set up to form the basis of an astrological chart, and how they relate to one another.

The basis of an astrological chart is a circle with the Earth at its centre. The circle is theoretically infinite in size, reaching far out into space beyond the Earth, and divided into 12 Houses like slices of a pie. Although the size of each House can be considered as infinite, each part carries the effects and experiences of the whole – just like a normal domestic house. The point at the centre of the circle represents the individual subject of the chart as the focus of all activity. This centre is where the various energies are controlled and combined. If combined successfully FOR THAT INDIVIDUAL (Birth Chart) there is a state of inner harmony resulting in physical and mental health.

There are several possible uses for an astrological chart where a clear beginning or "birth" can be identified – such as a new business or partnership. There is a separate branch of Astrology called "Mundane Astrology" that deals with countries and nations. Not having a clear "birth" date or time, the Ascendant for a country has been arrived at by observation over time. In this book we are only concerned with a Birth Chart (or "Natal Chart") of an individual person.

We use this basic chart structure for setting up the Personal Houses of a Birth Chart, as well as considering the Generic Houses of a single planet, or considering the relationship between any 2 planets.

BIRTH CHART : PERSONAL HOUSES

Personal Houses refer to the Houses of a Birth Chart. We note here that a Birth Chart can be interpreted at several different levels. You will see something of this from the different pictures and diagrams of this book. At another level, using "The Cycle of Growth", the Houses indicate the physical and psychological development of an individual from Conception to Death as well as the ability to transcend physical reality. There are others. By removing consideration of Signs and Planets from this chapter we portray an individual as the "raw clay" which will be worked on and moulded by life experiences on Earth. At this level we are all identical humans.

A Birth Chart is a map of the heavens showing the positions of planets at the time of birth of an individual person – more specifically that of the "first breath" - who is then the subject of the chart. The focus of activity is at the centre of a chart – which can be considered the axle of the "wheel" around which movement takes place. It is still - does not rotate itself - but nevertheless converts the energy into evolutionary motion or progress. The centre of a Birth Chart is the "Still Centre" of an individual.

Without adding any more information to the basic Birth Chart than is shown above it indicates where we are all the same. This is the basic structure, or template, of a Birth Chart and a human being. This is the 99.9% of DNA that makes us human and determines not only the structure of our human bodies and minds but how they develop over a lifetime. As we align the Birth Chart with the rest of the universe by determining the Rising Sign, and show the planet positions, it becomes more unique.

The figure above shows the basis of a Birth Chart with Earth at the centre and the surrounding space divided into Houses. The dividing lines between the Houses are called "Cusps". The single horizontal line is called " The Horizon " which defines the cusps of the 1st. and 7th. Houses – which are also the East (left) and West (right) points of the chart. You will see from this book that the House cusps at the 4 quarters of the chart have special significance, so they are given names.

- The 1st.House Cusp is "The Ascendant",
- The 7th. Is "The Descendant",
- The 4th. House Cusp is the "Lower Midheaven" (Immum Coeli)" and
- The 10th. is "The Midheaven (Medium Coeli)".

We are beginning to see that, to understand the Houses fully, we need to treat them as complementary pairs (not opposites !). If I use the word "opposite" anywhere in this book I mean "opposite by position".

THE ORIENTATION OF PERSONAL HOUSES

"Orient" means "East", so orienting the chart means aligning its East-West Horizon with that seen on Earth at the time and place of birth.

The first task in setting up a Birth Chart is determining the Ascendant, or Rising Sign, which symbolically aligns the event with those occurring in the rest of the universe at that same moment in time. This is the degree of the Zodiac Sign "rising" on the Eastern horizon (of the Earth location) at the time of the event. The Earth makes a complete rotation every 24 hours, and the Planets and Signs (seem to) rise and set in the same way as the Sun. With 12 Signs, each one is in the Ascendant for only 2 ½ hours a day. It is a problem that we often do not have an accurate birth time. In this case we set up a chart as accurately as possible – often using Noon or Sunrise. We can still examine the chart in terms of the planetary positions in the Zodiac, but are unable to make any observations concerning the physical events of Personal Transits (described later on). Despite this, by examining life events we are often able to "correct" (the birth time of) a chart to a greater or lesser degree.

In short, the Houses of an astrological chart, as a method of dividing or mapping space, and, referring to Earth, are always fixed in the same position, as shown in my diagram at the beginning of the chapter. We add the other details to that template. Through time we see the Sun continually rising in the Eastern Horizon (the Orient) and continuing until it sets. The chart therefore has similarities with the face of a clock. The Earth rotates anti-clockwise, so the Sun appears to rotate clockwise. It is exactly the same situation with the planets and Zodiac Signs which also seem to rise in the geographic East and set in the West. The East is symbolic as the position of the "rebirth" of the Sun, Moon, and planets each day. The Eastern point of a Birth Chart is the same as the geographic East at the time of birth, and defines the cusp of the 1st. House, which is also called the Ascendant as well as those of the other Houses. Having positioned our grid map we can now put the Sun, Moon, and other planets in the places they occupied at that time. The birth of an individual person is now oriented as an event in time and space, which is also related to the rest of the universe. A "rising star". A "star is born".

As an example, by setting up our chart for a particular time we know where the Sun is positioned. If we want to know approximately which direction is North on Earth we can point the hour hand of a clock at the Sun, when North is midway between it and 12 o'clock position (1 o'clock if the clock is set for Daylight Saving or Summer Time). We still need to do more accurate calculations, but this will serve to show how the Houses are oriented.

To begin with, we recognise Sunrise and Sunset, and, by definition, Noon, the 12 o'clock position, is the time when the Sun reaches its highest point in the sky. Having said that, to be perfectly accurate I should have said "seems to reach its highest point". We all know nowadays that the Sun is not actually moving, and its position in our sky is relative to the rotation of the Earth. This does not make our observations invalid, however (even the ancient ones). In Astrology we are always considering the RELATIVE positions of planets and the Earth. So it does not matter if we make our measurements from the Sun or the Earth. This is embodied in Einstein's Relativity Theory when it considers the relative positions of two moving bodies – such as moving trains, planets, or space ships.

In the figure below the Sun positions are shown for sunrise (Sun in the 1st.House) and noon (Sun in the 10th.House). This is true for any one day.

If we use the date of March 21st. when we know the Sun is in the Sign of Aries, the sunrise position gives an Aries Ascendant and Capricorn Midheaven, the noon position on the same day gives a Cancer Ascendant and Aries Midheaven (with the Sun still in Aries).

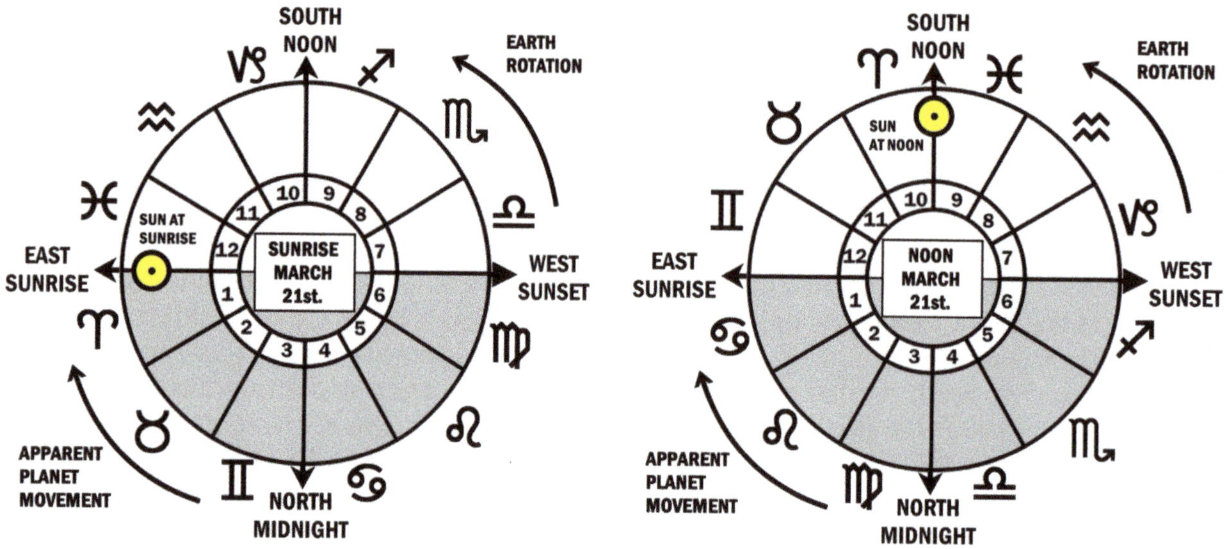

Figure 5: Aries Sun House positions for sunrise & noon March 21st.

THE PATTERN OF PERSONAL HOUSES IN MORE DETAIL

Here we deal with Birth Charts and the overall pattern of their Personal Houses. By comparing the Houses with one another we gain a better understanding of their separate functions. They are similar to, but not the same as, the meanings of the Signs. Clearly, both sets are influenced by the same 12 archetypes, but Houses refer to manifestation in physical forms in space (Earth. Physical Body. Mind), whereas Signs refer to different energy forms through time. Bearing in mind Einstein's statement that physical forms are also energy $E=MC^2$.

Taken as a set of 12, we can see that the Houses are numbered consecutively starting at the Ascendant, which is the cusp of the 1st. House, and continuing anti-clockwise. The Houses at opposite sides of the chart complement and balance one another. Later on, when we add Planets to the chart there is a state of imbalance produced which focuses energy into certain Houses.

Although for all practical purposes we can ignore it, I have to mention that this is a 2-dimensional representation of 3- dimensional space. The Earth and its surrounding space is actually spherical. What we are seeing is like an orange that has been cut in half and viewed from above. Because of this, as well as the tilt of the (imaginary) Earth's axis in relation to the Sun, there are various astrological house systems that vary the sizes of the 12 Houses. They still make a set of 12, but the slices of the "pie" are different sizes. "Opposite" (by position) Houses are the same size. We are using the "Equal House System" here. In my [CHARTS EXAMPLES] chapter I use the "Placidean" Unequal House System.

The overall principle is very similar to that of the imaginary lines of latitude and longitude used for navigating the Earth. The set of 12 Houses consists of 4 sets of 3 Triplicities, compared with the 12 Signs which are 3 sets of 4 Elements.

Although, for convenience, I tend to match the cusps of Houses and Signs in this book - this is rarely true in practice. For this to occur the cusp of a House must coincide with zero degrees of a Sign. I also put Aries as the Ascendant because its form of energy is similar to that of the 1st. House. An Aries Ascendant to a Birth Chart would give an easier general progress in life because the Houses and Signs would combine their energies in the most archetypally harmonious way. The individual would naturally work in harmony with the Time. The planet positions add another dimension of interpretation that might correspond with, or challenge, this activity.

Having set the chart up, we can begin to analyse it by ascribing meanings to the various areas. The first is a simple observation of the 4 Quadrants – which are each subdivided into 3 parts later on.

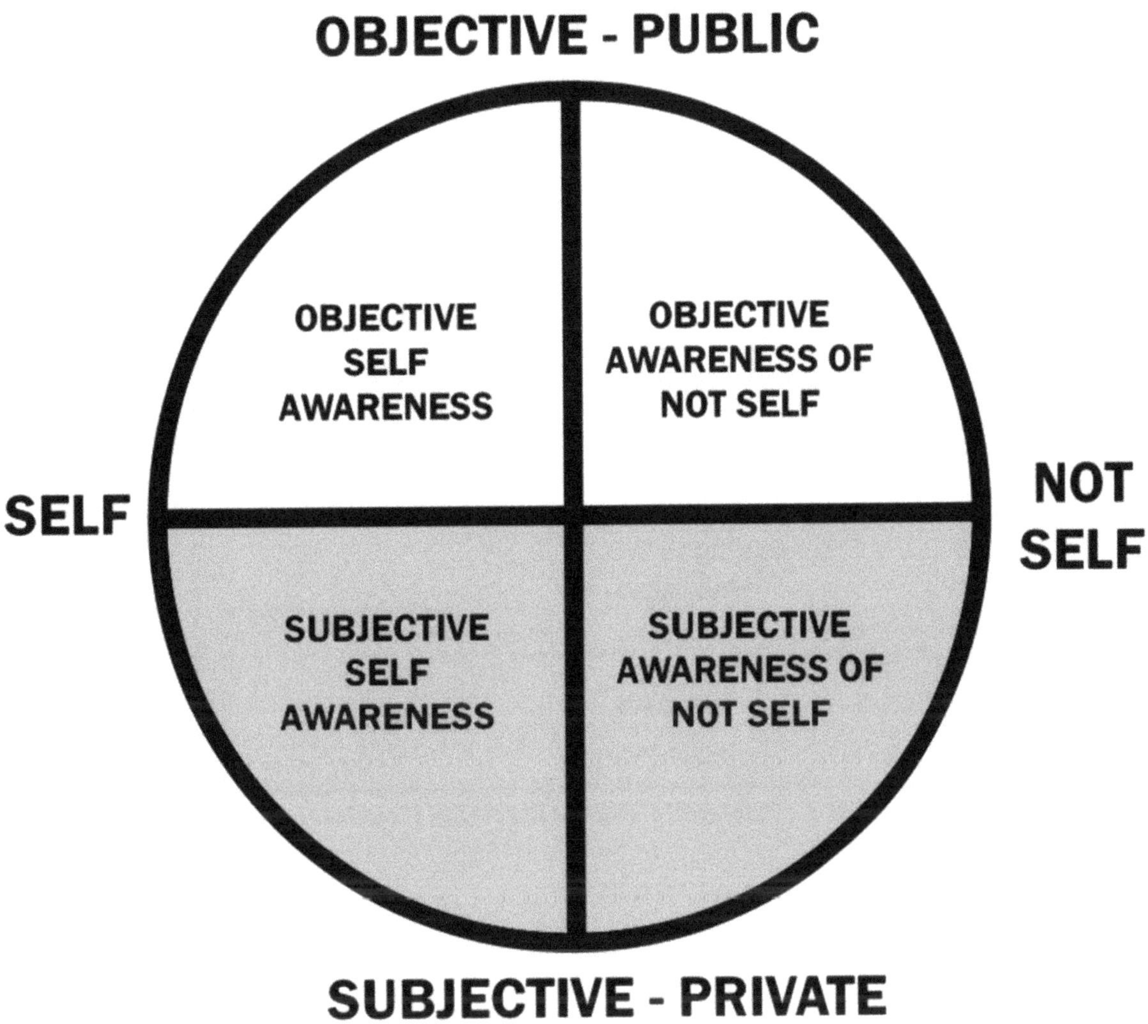

Figure 6 : The 4 Quadrants of a chart

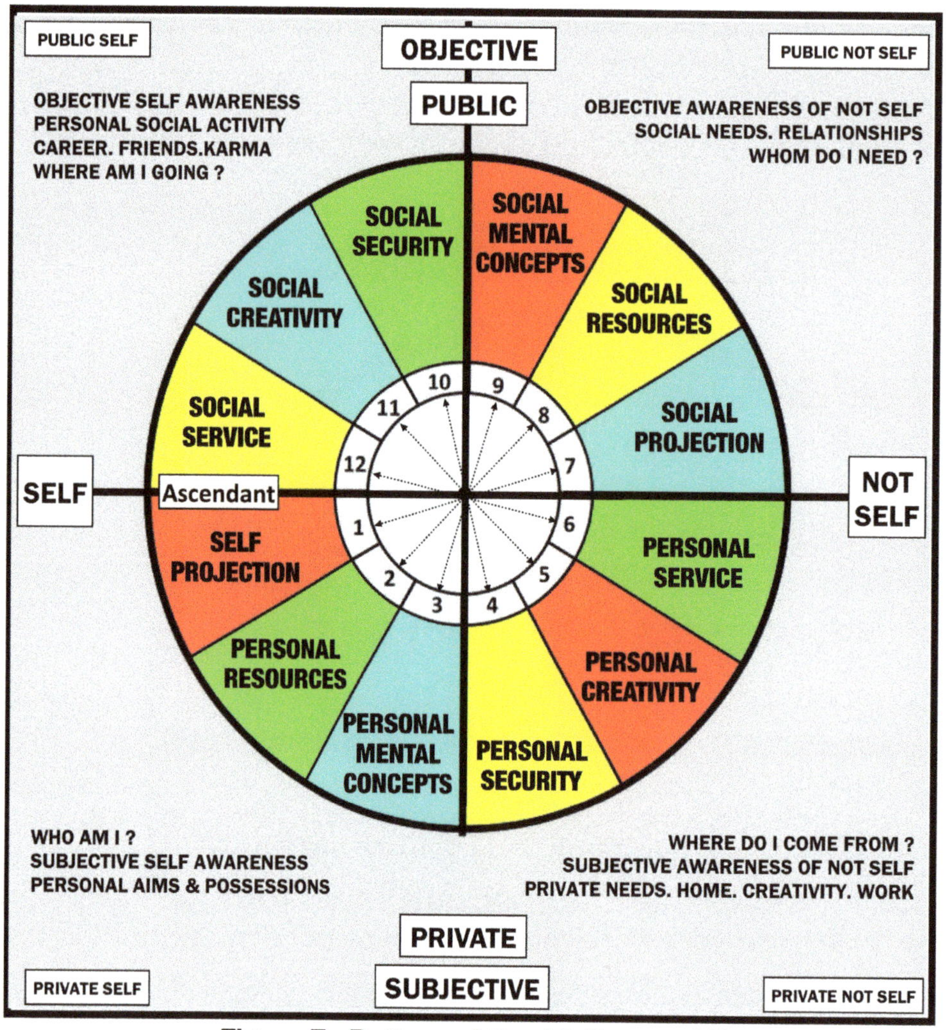

Figure 7 : Pattern of the 12 Personal Houses

BIRTH CHART HEMISPHERES : divisions by 2

There are 2 ways of dividing the chart circle (sphere) into hemispheres. We can see that each complements the other.

THE HORIZON

Dividing line EAST : WEST (SELF : NOT SELF)

Gives rise to hemispheres DAY : NIGHT. (OBJECTIVE : SUBJECTIVE) (PUBLIC : PRIVATE)

The East of a chart is on the left side.

The East – West horizontal Horizon line which forms the cusps of the 1st. and 7th. Houses is a representation of the Earth's horizon which separates the earth below and sky above. It represents the unique personal outlook, or world view, of the subject of the chart. What is near and what is at a distance. Our Private Life and Public Life. Above the Horizon is day time, where the journey of the Sun consciousness from sunrise to sunset brings us awareness of the external world. Below the horizon is night time when Sun/Moon consciousness brings attention to our inner world.

THE LOWER MIDHEAVEN - MIDHEAVEN LINE

Dividing line NORTH : SOUTH. (SUBJECTIVE : OBJECTIVE) (PRIVATE : PUBLIC)

Gives rise to hemispheres SELF : NOT SELF.

The line divides the chart into left and right hemispheres. The main focus of the left hemisphere is on the Ascendant and the 1st.House. This indicates how the individual projects his or herself into life, as at birth. It indicates the natural way for that person to "plant seeds" of new projects and experiences. The activities of the Houses in that hemisphere are more or less under one's personal control.

The Houses in the right hemisphere are those which require co-operation with other people and the environment.

BIRTH CHART QUADRANTS : division by 4 sets of 3 Houses

Each Quadrant contains a "Triplicity" of Houses which have similar properties to Cardinal, Fixed, and Mutable Signs. They are Angular (Active. Initiating "Creator"), Succedent (Resisting. "Preserver"), and Cadent (Changing. Adapting. "Destroyer").

Applying both hemisphere divisions together divides the chart into 4 quadrants, each containing 3 Houses. I have deliberately not described each House in the narrative. My aim is to describe the basic House structure in as simple terms as possible. You will probably note some seeming anomalies which will hopefully be clarified and explained in the chapters about the separate Cycle of Growth stages.

QUADRANT 1 : SUBJECTIVE SELF AWARENESS (Houses 1 to 3)

Symbolically relates to the 3 months of Spring - Aries, Taurus, Gemini.

The Quadrant is concerned with development from physical birth to 3 years 6 months of age when a child is weaned from its mother, develops body and mind, and learns to control them. It is indicative of the inbuilt abilities and talents waiting to develop.

QUADRANT 2 : SUBJECTIVE AWARENESS OF NOT SELF (Houses 4 to 6)

Symbolically relates to the 3 months of Summer – Cancer, Leo, Virgo

The Quadrant is concerned with development during ages 3 to 23 years beginning with growing awareness of the world outside that of home and family, which enables the awareness of one's self as a separate individual – and which requires the development of a Persona, or "mask" to become an actor on the stage of life, where it is not appropriate to reveal all of one's inner self. There is the development of an Ego which can say "I am".

QUADRANT 3: OBJECTIVE AWARENESS OF NOT SELF (Houses 7 to 9)

Symbolically relates to the 3 months of Autumn – Libra, Scorpio, Sagittarius.

The 7th. House Cusp is opposite that of the 1st. House cusp of Birth. It is the end of the "outward journey" into life and the beginning of preparation for death and return to our Source. The 7th. House is that of Partners.

The Quadrant includes the time of life from 23 years of age to Death. To develop further, and to reproduce so that our genes survive our physical death, we need the co-operation of others outside our self.

QUADRANT 4 : OBJECTIVE SELF AWARENESS (Houses 10 to 12)

Symbolically relates to the 3 Winter months and Capricorn, Aquarius, Pisces.

This Quadrant takes us out of the realms of personal growth and into that of a wider society, and mankind as a whole. In terms of "The Cycle of Growth" it has 2 functions. Firstly, as applied to the time of Gestation, it includes the time of life from Conception to Birth and the development of the human body as a vehicle which is determined by past human evolution. At another level, as following after the previous Quadrant that includes Death, it covers our Transcendence of earthly concerns. This is always relative to the individual concerned. For example, it may relate to the individual gaining a social overview by running a business, becoming active in politics, or studying science or religion.

In traditional terms, at the beginning of the Quadrant we have the 10th. House as an indicator of the power we have to control others. It is the House of Career as well as being the place where we come into full public view. In "The Cycle of Growth", and the Birth Chart, this is "The Peak" position. The position of the Sun at the height of its power at mid-day. The point is that, in life, such times are transitory. There is always a decline afterwards. The decline is indicated by the activities of the 11th. and 12th. Houses – which return us to the 1st. House Birth Ascendant position.

In human and agricultural terms, the 10th.House is the final "harvest time" of all our efforts since 1st.House "seed time" and preparation for Winter decline of activity in preparation for a new cycle beginning at Spring.

TRANSCENDENCE

Another factor to consider is that the traditional meanings need to be updated. Each planet has a compatible energy relationship with certain Signs and Houses which tend to reinforce and support its activity. With others its expression is limited or restricted.

Traditional Astrology gives "Rulership" of the 10th. and 11th. Houses to Saturn as being the most compatible planet with its concern for bringing order and structure to life. It gives rulership of the 12th. House to Jupiter – with its principle of bringing Expansion and Growth to whatever it comes into contact.

Since then we have the discovery of planets beyond Saturn which are invisible to the (physical) naked eye, and which required advanced technology to discover. These are Uranus, Neptune, and Pluto. Saturn still rules the 10th. House, but Uranus and Neptune have been given rulership of the 11th. and 12th. Houses respectively. When we apply this to our Transcendent Quadrant this makes sense. To begin with, the attitude of modern Astrologers is that the discovery of these planets is a sign that modern humans have reached a stage in evolution where we can, if desired, respond to the energies that they express.

In the 11th.House there is a symbolic form of struggle between traditional Saturn and evolutionary Uranus. If Saturn wins, Jupiter will control the 12th.House and the next cycle will be the same as the current one. If Uranus wins, Neptune controls the 12th. House and acts to clear away the remnants and memories of the past in preparation for the planting of new "seeds".

To understand the Transcendent activity in human terms, we can consider that traditionally the 10th. House time of Capricorn (Peak. Harvest) each year is that of making "New Year Resolutions" (Uranus) for the future based upon one's previous experience and achievements. To achieve those aims usually requires overcoming inner and/or outer resistance (Saturn). If Saturn wins, we fail to achieve our new aims.

PERSONAL HOUSES AND PLANETS

The orbits of the planets and the Earth are all concentric, with the Sun as central point, within very close limits. The orbits are actually elliptical rather than circular, so the planets do not travel at exactly the same speed through the Zodiac all the time, but the calculations take this into account. This means that the astrological "map" is a good representation of what would actually be seen from a view point above the North Pole of the Earth. It is not accurate when considering the relative distances in space between the planets, but, again, for practical purposes, this can be ignored. We are only interested in the position of a planet by House and Sign.

The next step in setting up our chart is to insert the planets in their positions relative to that of the Earth at that moment in time. For that we need to make a lot of complicated calculations, which a computer nowadays does in a second. In the past it might have taken me an hour using various tables, with the ever present possibility of making errors. We also need to have a knowledge of the astrological Zodiac Signs. I am leaving that stage until the next chapter [ZODIAC SIGNS].

SIGNS OF THE ZODIAC

The Signs of the Zodiac are different forms of expression of the basic Solar source of energy which contains them all. White light contains all possible colours. In this book they are described simply as they are used to map the positions of Planets into an Astrological chart.

The 12 Zodiac Signs are considered as 4 Elemental sets (Fire, Earth, Air, Water) of 3 Qualities (Cardinal, Fixed, Mutable).

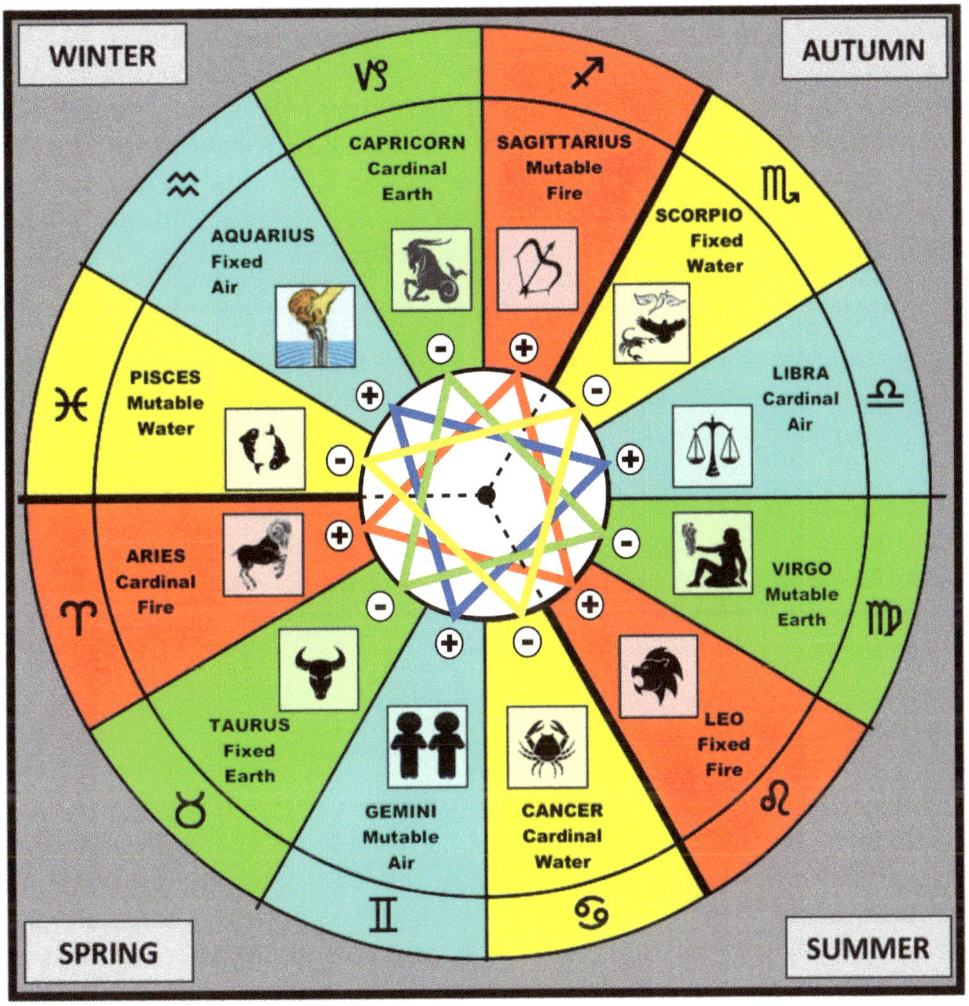

Figure 8 : Astrology - Zodiac Signs

BIRTH CHART HOUSE & SIGN RELATIONSHIPS

The 24 hour rotation of The Earth gives a new Zodiac Sign rising on the Eastern Horizon (The Ascendant) every 2 hours. The 1st. House of a Birth Chart is always on the Eastern Horizon, and its relationship with a Sign is fixed at the time of birth.

The 12 Zodiac Signs relate to Time and various forms of energy, whereas the 12 Houses of a chart relate to Space, and the physical manifestation on Earth –no Sign is more or less "spiritual" than another. To become a whole individual we eventually have to master the abilities and problems brought by each one – perhaps over several lifetimes. A Birth Chart – with the Sun Sign as a main focus - is an indicator of what we have come to learn in the current lifetime. The Signs are related to the annual cycle of 12 months.

The diagram above is similar to an Astrological chart but has the outer Zodiac Signs extended to show more detail. In effect, the outer Zodiac circle extends to infinity. The white circle at the centre represents Earth and would normally show the 12 Houses of the chart. The central Earth circle defines the orientation of the chart around which the Signs (appear to) rotate clockwise, or rise and set, like the Sun, with time – so defining the months of the year. The Signs are here shown in their positions as at sunrise at the Spring Equinox each year which resets the "Zodiac Clock" to zero degrees of Aries.

It is important to note that nowadays the Zodiac Signs bear no relationship with the star patterns of the heavens. They were set at around 2000 BC when Astrology as we know it today was born. Due to the Precession of the Equinoxes caused by the Earth wobbling on its axis we now have Aquarius rising at the Spring Equinox instead of Aries. People who do not understand Astrology say that this makes it invalid – ignoring the fact that the Signs refer to LIFE ON EARTH - our annual Seasons and Months have not changed. We have to realise that The Signs are set by TIME rather than SPACE – and are related to our annual Calendar, which was originally concerned with agriculture at a time where reading and writing were practically non-existent. The "Zodiac Calendar" is reset to Zero degrees of Aries at sunrise on the day of the Spring Equinox when day and night are equal. This is similar to the divisions of Earth by imaginary lines of Latitude and Longitude.

4 ELEMENTS – FIRE, EARTH, AIR, WATER

The 4 inner triangles indicate the relative positions of the 3 Signs which relate to each of the 4 Elements. Fire (Red. Positive), Earth (Green. Negative), Air (Blue. Positive), and Water (Yellow. Negative).

POLARITIES – POSITIVE OR NEGATIVE

The mathematical Plus and Minus signs in the diagram indicate the Polarity of the Zodiac Signs. Fire and Air are Positive, Earth and Water are Negative. We note that complementary Signs on the opposite sides of the chart are of the same polarity. There is some conflict there because like polarity repels – opposite attracts.

If we add up the effects of the Zodiac Signs through a complete cycle, the sum total is Zero. The mixture of colours returns to White.

THE 3 OCTAVES

The white centre circle is also divided into 3 parts with dotted lines. Each part contains a Sign of each Element in the same order. This is an indication of how the Signs' archetypes relate to the 3 Octaves of the Logarithmic Timescale of "The Cycle of Growth" in the (fixed position) Houses of a Birth Chart. One again, they will only coincide with the Signs as here once a year at sunrise of the day of the Spring Equinox.

3 QUALITIES – CARDINAL, FIXED, MUTABLE

Whereas Houses are mainly treated as 4 sets of 3, the Signs are arranged as 3 sets of 4 Elements in the order Fire, Earth, Air, Water. Each Element has 3 Qualities, or modes of action - Cardinal, Fixed, and Mutable. The diagram shows that a Cardinal Sign is followed by a Fixed Sign, then a Mutable Sign (of different Elements). In this arrangement, based on (sets of) Number 3, the 3 Quality types of Elements (Cardinal, Fixed, Mutable) are similar in activity to the 3 Triplicity types of the Houses (Angular, Succedent, Cadent).

Father : Cardinal Signs (Angular Houses) initiate activity.

Mother : Fixed Signs (Succedent Houses) tend to resist activity (inertia) modify and organise the initial impulse.

Child : Mutable ("Changeable") Signs (Cadent Houses) are the result of the combination.

In Numerology, Number 3 is a discrete "set". It consists of 3 modes which exist (repetitively) in turn in such triplicities as Action, Reaction, Result - Creator, Preserver, Destroyer – Thesis, Antithesis, Synthesis - (etc.). These are examples of how an Archetype (in this case Number 3) can manifest in numerous "forms".

THE BIRTH CHART

Although the House positions in an astrological chart are fixed, the set of Sign positions varies depending on the time and place the chart is set up for. If you refer to the Birth Chart of Lady Diana Spencer [CHARTS EXAMPLES] you will see that she has the Mutable Fire Sign Sagittarius rising on the cusp of her 1st. House (Ascendant) instead of the archetypal Cardinal Fire Sign Aries in the diagram above. The departure from the archetypal arrangement (which is common to most of us) brings difficulties in life from the need to consciously control and rebalance the energies involved when undertaking personal projects or activities. Having a Fire Sign rising is useful in promoting one's personal activities, but Mutable (Changeable) Sagittarius makes it difficult to focus the energy, whereas archetypal Cardinal (Initiating) Aries has complete focus and is not too bothered with side issues (Me-Me). The art of chart analysis consists of taking such things into account for each House\Sign\Planet position.

CONCLUSION

For the purposes of this book we need to go no further. It is enough to understand that the Zodiac Signs are used to accurately specify the positions of the Planets at any particular time – past, present, or future in relationship to Earth. There is more detail in my book "The Cycle of Growth".

PLANET TRANSITS AND HOW TO USE THEM

Having set up a Birth Chart, which becomes fixed in time and space, we then consider the movements of the Planets afterwards in relationship to the chart.

The Birth Chart can be considered as our personal inner "Nature" whilst the Transits are external influences -"Nurture".

This book is not concerned with day to day experiences. It focuses on the structure of a whole lifetime. We therefore ignore the faster moving planets and focus on the 12 year cycle of Jupiter and the 30 year cycle of Saturn. The 84 year cycle of Uranus is mentioned as it is connected, at a personal level, with the Jungian Process of Individuation – however, knowledge of this subject is limited at present. The orbits of Neptune (165 years) and Pluto (247 years) affect so many people in a similar way that they too are beyond the scope of this book. They affect whole generations of people.

We use the Birth Chart of Lady Diana Spencer as an example.

WE EMPHASISE THAT EACH TRANSIT PLANET CAN BE CONSIDERED IN RELATION TO ITS PERSONAL HOUSE TRANSIT CYCLE AND GENERIC HOUSE TRANSIT CYCLE AT ONE AND THE SAME TIME.

Another important consideration is that :-

AFTER CYCLE OF GROWTH STAGE 1 (SEED) THE CONTINUED DEVELOPMENT OF A NEW CYCLE IS ENTIRELY DEPENDENT ON OUR PERSONAL ACTIONS THEREAFTER. THE PRINCIPLE IS EXACTLY THE SAME AS ASTROLOGY ORIGINALLY BEING USED AS A CALENDAR TO PLOUGH, SOW, AND REAP, AT THE RIGHT TIMES. IF THE SEED DIES THERE WILL BE NO HARVEST. THIS IS A MATTER OF CONSCIOUSNESS AND WILL.

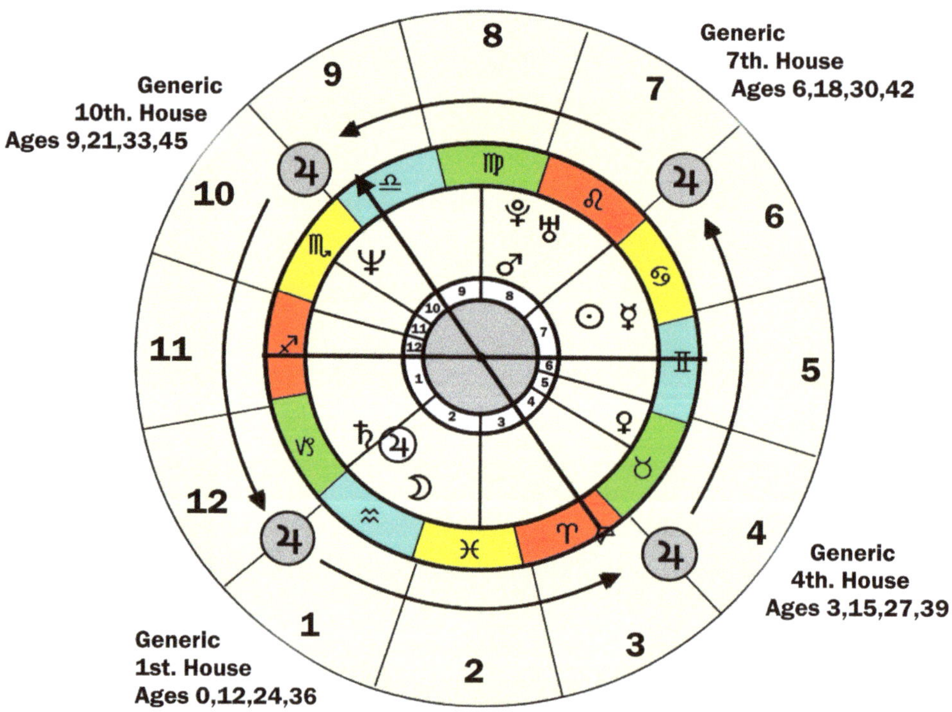

Figure 9: The Generic Cycle of Jupiter diagram

THE CYCLE OF JUPITER DIAGRAM

1. The chart consists of 4 concentric circles. Although they are shown separately, they interpenetrate one another :-
   i. The inner circle of the Birth Chart which represents the Earth, and the individual person (coloured grey). This is the "Still Centre" where all activity is brought to focus.
   ii. The circle of Personal Houses of the Birth Chart which is fixed at the time of birth.
   iii. The circle of Zodiac Signs which consist of different forms of energy and enable us to locate the Planet positions.
   iv. The circle of Generic Houses of Jupiter, which is outside the Birth Chart and is specific to that planet only.
2. There may appear to be a slight disorientation of Houses. This is because I use the Placidean Unequal Personal House system for a Birth Chart and the 12 Generic Houses are each 30 degrees.
3. To define the Generic Transit Houses of a Planet we take its position in the Birth Chart and mark off 12 x 30 degree divisions from there.
4. Although detailed analysis would require consideration of the Zodiac Signs, here they are only used for locating the planet(s). The 1st. Generic House of each Planet takes on the attributes of Aries, the 2nd. Taurus – and so on.
5. In the case of this particular Birth Chart, because Jupiter and Saturn are close to one another ("Conjunction Aspect") we can consider them as having the same Generic Houses. Apart from the House meanings they are not identical, however. Jupiter has a 12 year cycle and Saturn a 30 year cycle.
6. The transit of each Generic Jupiter House takes around 1 year. This is variable because there are periods of "retrogradation" when planets appear to move backwards in the Zodiac Circle, and then go "Direct" again. It is this that led astrologers to discover that the Earth is not the centre of our Solar System. In the case of Jupiter, the Earth orbits the Sun 12 times to Jupiter's 1, so it catches up with and overtakes Jupiter every year. Because Earth seems stationary to us, Jupiter seems to go backwards as Earth overtakes it – rather like cars on a motorway.
7. The 1st., 4th., 7th. and 10th. House cusps have special emphasis as "crisis points" when events are triggered. This is the same for Personal House transits, and Generic House transits. The diagram shows some of the ages at which they occur.
8. As recognition that "The Cycle of Growth" refers to all cycles, the principles here can be applied to any Planet, and any life time. We can all recognise the Spring, Summer, Autumn, and Winter of a human lifetime – which is only a single example.

PERSONAL TRANSITS

Personal Transits refer to the position of a transiting Planet to the Houses of a Birth Chart. In the diagram above, Jupiter is located in Diana's 2nd. birth House, so it continues to orbit her Personal 2nd.House immediately afterwards – which is Generic Jupiter's 1st. Generic House. For example :-

1. During her second year of age Jupiter enters her Personal 4th. House, but Jupiter does not reach its Generic 4th. House until she is 3 years of age. This is repeated every 12 years.
2. The difference is clearer at ages 6, 18, 30, and so on, because as Generic Jupiter enters its Generic 7th. House it begins transiting Diana's Personal 8th. House.

Personal House Transits are interpreted in exactly the same way as Generic House Transits. This is examined in more detail in "The Cycle of Growth". So, for example, any 1st. House transit refers to Cycle of Growth Stage 1 (Seed) when seeds are sown for new beginnings. Whether that seed has any effect or not is a matter for individual consciousness and Will. Our natural tendency is to ignore new trends and continue our habitual lifestyle unless forced to change by circumstances. If we continue to plant the same seeds we eventually reap the same harvest.

GENERIC TRANSITS

We have seen that :-

1. *Generic Houses refer to* ***PLANET ORBITS*** *and are not the same as Birth Chart Houses unless the planet is located in the 1st. House of a Birth Chart. However, "The Cycle of Growth" meanings of Personal and Generic Houses are identical.*
2. *Each Planet has its own set of Generic Houses depending on its position in a Birth Chart – which is the starting place of its Generic Cycle for the person concerned.*
3. *"The Cycle of Growth" demonstrates that these same principles apply to any cycle and any evolutionary (growth) process – such as the evolution of planets and mankind since The Big Bang.*
4. *The Generic Cycles of planets are the same for all of us. The only difference is the starting point in the Birth Chart. We therefore do not need a Birth Chart to define their effect on us, only their position compared with the starting point – which is solely dependent on our age.*

The Generic Transit cycles of each planet are what makes human development the same. Even though the planets in our Birth Chart may be in different Houses to those of other people, they are in the same Generic House positions at the same ages and we tend to have similar experiences and growth stages at around the same age. During its transit cycle a planet will make every possible aspect (angular relationship) - harmonious or otherwise - with every other planet in the birth chart as well as the other transiting planets – so the sum total is Zero for each cycle.

The Moon orbiting the Earth has a Transit Cycle of 28 days. The Sun, Mercury and Venus, being inside the orbit of the Earth, can be considered as having a 1 year Transit Cycle. These transits tend to "fire off" events set up by the slower planets. Their transits make every possible aspect with Birth Chart planets and other transit planets every 12 months.

Mars has a 2 year cycle, Jupiter 12 years, Saturn 30 years, Uranus 84 years, Neptune 165 years, Pluto 247 years. Neptune and Pluto, because of their slow movement, are in the same Sign for several years and therefore affect whole generations of people in the same way. The Uranus cycle matches what we are beginning to expect as a whole life term of 84 years and is connected with the Jungian concept of Individuation. My main interests in this book are the cycles of Jupiter and Saturn. Because they repeat during a lifetime we can compare actual life events at times when their positions are the same.

THE GENERIC "MONTHLY HOROSCOPE" AND "ANNUAL DIARY"

We are all familiar with the annual celebration of our "Birthday" – which is the Generic return of the Sun to its position when we were born. The Sun has a 1 year Generic Cycle and it is this that is used to calculate our Monthly (or daily) Horoscope without needing a Birth Chart. We know which Sign the Sun was in when we were born, and this sets the Ascendant cusp of our 1st. Generic Sun House to that Sign, the cusp of our 2nd. Generic House to the following Sign – and so on.

The Generic House of the Transiting Sun and its meaning provide a focus of activity. The aspects made by the other planets to the Sun provide additional meanings.

The diagram below shows an Annual Diary for someone born on May 27th. It indicates some important ideas related to "The Cycle of Growth".

1. Everything on Earth begins with an idea or "conception" in somebody's mind. Although we start The Personal Life Diary at the point of physical birth, we were still the result of a conception from our parents and its later development. "The Cycle of Growth" does take into account the experiences we have whilst in the womb (via our mother), and which scientific research has shown to have a greater effect than first realised.
2. All cyclic calculations start at the birth position. So for birthdays after the 15th. day of the month events could occur in the following month.

Month	Stage	Meaning	Event
January 27 2014	9	CONCEPTION. IDEAS FOR FUTURE GROWTH Wider viewpoint."New year resolutions".	
February 27 2014	10	PEAK. HARVEST The final result of the PREVIOUS cycle	
March 27 2014	11	DISCONTENT. DESIRE FOR CHANGE Decline of interest	
April 27 2014	12	WITHDRAWAL. CONFINEMENT Preparation for a new phase	
May 27	1	BIRTHDAY SEED OPPORTUNITY New beginnings - or repetition of the past	
June 27 2014	2	GERMINATION Spending time, money, & effort	
July 27 2014	3	EXPERIMENT. COMMUNICATION Testing on the "family"	
August 27 2014	4	TRANSPLANTING. NEW ROOTS Spreading the word	
September 27 2014	5	POWER. CREATIVITY Acting out a new role	
October 27 2014	6	HEALTH. SERVICE TO SELF Practical re-adjustment	
November 27 2014	7	PARTNERS. NEW SOCIAL CONTACTS Seeking help	
December 27 2014	8	INTERCOURSE. DEATH. SYNERGY The sum is greater than the parts	
January 27 2015	9	CONCEPTION. IDEAS FOR FUTURE GROWTH Wider viewpoint."New year resolutions".	
February 27 2015	10	PEAK. HARVEST The final result of THIS cycle	
March 27 2015	11	DISCONTENT. DESIRE FOR CHANGE Decline of interest	
April 27 2015	12	WITHDRAWAL. CONFINEMENT Preparation for a new phase	

Figure 10 : Annual Life Diary

INTERPRETATION OF THE STAGES

The diagram below summarises the symbolic activities of the 12 Generic Houses which are identical with the 12 stages of the annual agricultural calendar. The "crisis" stages coincide with the Spring and Autumn Equinoxes, and the Summer and Winter Solstices.

The actual time of the activity at a personal level depends on the Generic position of the planet related to its position time of birth. Each planet has its own cycle which may or may not match our Calendar. Each Generic Planet Cycle starts at the time of birth. We can therefore see how certain times of life their activities may conflict with, or support, one another.

Although a planet can be in any Zodiac Sign at the time of birth, the activities during transits of the Generic 1st.House is symbolically linked with the Sign of Aries, the 2nd. House with Taurus – and so on.

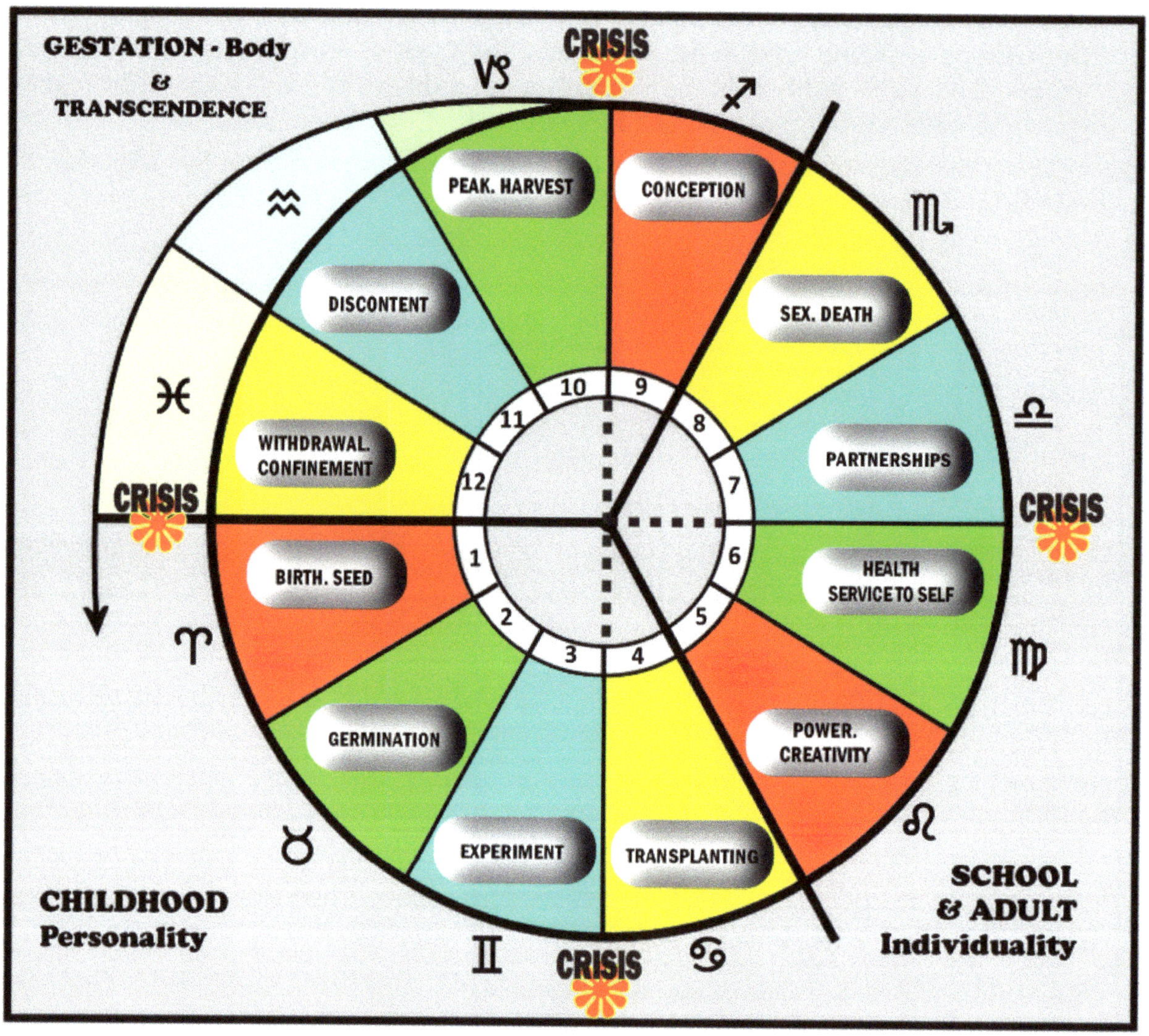

Figure 11 : Generic Houses Summary Diagram

The diagram shows the correspondence between the division of the 12 Stages into the 3 x 4 Stages of The Cycle of Growth and the 4 x 3 Stages of Personal Birth Chart Houses and Generic Planet Stages.

THE 1ST. OCTAVE OF "THE CYCLE OF GROWTH"
AND THE 4TH. QUARTER OF GENERIC TRANSITS

The Cycle of Growth years of age here refer to the "Growth of Personality" stages of Psychology (Erik Erikson) which match the Astrological Logarithmic Timescale.

"The Cycle of Growth" shows that the real beginning of a cycle is at Cycle of Growth Stage 9 (Conception). This is the beginning of the 1st. Octave of The Cycle of Growth, and is archetypally linked with :-

1. The 9th. House of a cycle
2. The 9th. Zodiac Sign of Sagittarius (Mutable Fire) and its time of year.
3. The Immaculate Conception of Jesus and preparation for his birth which is celebrated later at the time of Christmas (the birth of the SON).
4. The Winter Solstice (the rebirth of the SUN) and its promise of a new Spring to come. A time for planting new seeds.
5. The (sexless) "immaculate conception" of an idea in our mind.
6. The conception of "New Year Resolutions".
7. The "Big Bang" of the creation of our universe out of No-Thing.
8. Number 1

The point is that all material things begin with an abstract idea in the mind which does not materialise until more work is done. "In the beginning was the Word". This is mentioned because there is a need to contrast the abstract principles (archetypes) of The Cycle of Growth with the more down-to-earth activities which follow.

THE 1ST. QUARTER – PHYSICAL BIRTH

We are now at Cycle of Growth Stage 1 (Seed) – which is the beginning of Spring when seeds which have been hidden in the ground over Winter begin to take material form in human consciousness. In human terms, the child now emerges from the womb.

THE GENERIC PLANET CYCLES BEGIN HERE, AT THE MOMENT OF BIRTH.

We all, therefore, have our own inner "clock", or relationship with universal Time.

We now apply archetypal "agricultural" principles to our earthy activities. In terms of Planet Personal and Generic Transits the principles are identical – it is just that each Stage takes a different amount of time. In the case of the Sun each Stage takes 1 month, for Jupiter the 12 stages each take 1 year, Saturn's stages take 2 ½ years. I have mentioned that this varies slightly depending on the retrograde motion of planets. With each planet having 2 cycle effects, as well as inter-relating with one another in co-operation or opposition, we begin to see how the seeming complexity of human behaviour is based on simple "rules".

WE NOTE THAT THE BEGINNING OF A QUARTER IS THE MOST LIKELY TIME FOR EVENTS TO OCCUR. THAT IS THE 1ST. 4TH. 7TH. AND 10TH. STAGES. THE INTERVENING PERIODS ARE THAT OF DEVELOPMENT AND PREPARATION FOR THE NEXT MAJOR CHANGE. THIS ASSUMES THAT SOME ACTION IS, IN FACT, TAKEN – OTHERWISE THERE IS NO CHANGE.

Although the actual birth can be at any time of the year, the Generic 1st. Quarter symbolises the "rebirth" time of Spring which creates its own division of cycles into 4 sets of 3 Houses & related Signs. At the beginning of life this is the birth of a physical child after the time of gestation in the womb and its subsequent development in "The Garden of Eden" of protected family life. The Stage is repeated each time a planet returns to its position at the time of birth.

Although a planet can be in any Zodiac Sign at the time of birth, the activities during transits of the Generic 1st.House are symbolically linked with the Sign of Aries, the 2nd. House with Taurus – and so on.

1st. HOUSE TRANSIT – BIRTH. SEED TIME. SEEDS FOR FUTURE GROWTH

Aries : The Ram. Cardinal (Active. Initiating Fire. Spring)

Rebirth. Beginning of a new cycle. New interests. New ideas.

What was conceived at the Stage 9 time of Conception becomes a more tangible, physical reality. “The child” is born.

On entry into its 1st.House the planet has completed its transit of the 12th. House which has the function of clearing away the debris of the past to make room for new life. The 12th. House is mainly concerned with psychological preparation and rest, so there may or may not be actual events occurring during that time. This corresponds with the withdrawal and confinement of an expectant mother just prior to birth.

WHAT FOLLOWS IS NOT NECESSARILY WHAT WILL HAPPEN. WE HUMANS TEND TO EXIST IN A STATE OF INERTIA IN THE FACE OF CHANGE. IF NEW SEEDS ARE NOT SOWN, AND NEW OPPORTUNITIES NOT GRASPED, WE WILL SOW THE SAME SEEDS AND REAP THE SAME HARVEST AS THE PREVIOUS CYCLE. SOMETIMES WE HAVE TO GO THROUGH THE SAME EXPERIENCES SEVERAL TIMES BEFORE WE REALISE THAT THEY ARE DETRIMENTAL TO US. WHAT STOPS GROWING WILL DIE.

THE CYCLES TEND TO PRESENT OPPORTUNITIES RATHER THAN FORCED CHANGE. THE PRINCIPLE MOTIVATION OF THE CYCLE OF GROWTH IS THE DEVELOPMENT OF WILL BASED ON MAKING DECISIONS AND CARRYING THEM OUT.

This is a time of POSSIBILITY for new growth which may or may not be developed. “The child” may be stillborn or die from lack of attention.

This is the beginning of a new cycle. Some decision is, or has been, made - consciously or unconsciously - which will establish future direction. This becomes the "seed". There may be the need to re-organise one’s life in the face of current changes. The “child” is born.

At this time it is advisable to keep one’s ideas to one’s self. "Seeds", like babies, need to develop where they are protected. If revealed too soon they are likely to be distorted or destroyed. Nothing is clear yet. If one’s own doubts and fears are not resolved inwardly they may not be expressed in the proper way. At this time the aim is to do as little as possible. Any actions are likely to concern the old cycle, resulting in the same seeds being sown again. The new cycle will then be a repetition of the earlier one.

CYCLE OF GROWTH STAGE 1 (SEED)

This is the beginning of the 2nd. Octave of The Cycle of Growth. The 1st. Octave refers to our development in the womb. The Stage refers to the actual time of birth of a child. Having developed “in secret” it is ready to be “planted” in the Earth to develop and grow further.

2nd. HOUSE TRANSIT – GERMINATION. USING PERSONAL RESOURCES

Taurus : The Bull. Fixed (Controlled) Earth. Resources. Money. The human body.

“Seed" ideas develop and become practical. There is a need to reassess use of resources of time, money, and effort to take the new trend into account as it begins to take root in the “subsoil” of the past. Failure to take into account this, and other stages, will mean repetition of the past.

This is a test of responsible reorganisation and management of all one’s resources relative to the new area of growth. Providing support to the “new born”. Not a time of much external activity. As one moves away from this phase there will be need to spend time, money, and effort, in relationship to the new possibilities that have been revealed, however limited this might be to begin with. One may find that new talents or abilities are revealed that require attention.

During the time Saturn was transiting my 1st. Personal Birth Chart House (Seed) I was thinking about the possibility of writing a book.

THE CYCLE OF GROWTH STAGE 2 (GERMINATION)

The child learns to control the physical body and begins to develop an inner, psychological "image" of the world outside.

During the 2 ½ years it took me to write "The Cycle of Growth" Saturn was transiting my 2nd. Personal Birth Chart House (Germination).

3rd. HOUSE TRANSIT – EXPERIMENT. TRIAL & ERROR. COMMUNICATION

Gemini : The Twins. Mutable (Changeable) Air. Mind.

Testing the theory. Caution. Trial & Error. Study. Experiment. Mental activity.

Communication with those close.

The seed begins to sprout. This is a time of experimentation. There is now the need to take some tentative action to see what sort of reaction one gets from others around. One must expect some negativity from those close because their lives will be affected too. They may not be ready for the possible changes required. There may also be the need to adapt one's "product" to the realities of social needs. This requires "market research". It is unlikely that what you have to offer has global appeal, so you need to find your target consumer. Also to discover where your focus of activity should be. This may require investigating areas of society that you may not have considered before.

There may be the need for some form of study or reading of books. Perhaps communication in speech or writing. This is the home of Scientific method. Experiment. Trial and error. Testing your "product". At this stage expect more failures than successes.

As I write this, Saturn is beginning its 2 ½ year transit of my 3rd. Personal Birth Chart House. Having completed "The Cycle of Growth" I realised that getting a book published and sold was not straightforward. Having shown it to some friends and done some research I decided that, to begin with, a smaller book would be a more viable proposition to practice on.

THE CYCLE OF GROWTH STAGE 3 (EXPERIMENT. COMMUNICATION)

Having learned to control its body, this is the age of mental development. At around 2 to 3 years of age the child learns the "rules" and begins to question the parents.

2ND. QUARTER - SUMMER

4th. HOUSE TRANSIT – CRISIS. TRANSPLANTING.

We have to note that the 3 Stages related to Water Signs are concerned with dissolution of the past to make a new future. The 12th House before the beginning of a new cycle. The 4th. House leaving the "home" or place of inner development, and The 8th. House of Sex and Death in preparation for contact with broader principles. They bring times of Transition.

Cancer : The Crab. The Shell. Cardinal (Active. Initiating) Water.

Break from the past. New roots. New "home". Personal foundations. A step forward.

The new plant (or child) requires strong roots. This may require transplanting to allow necessary space to grow further. Greater security. A bigger "shell" than the original. Preparing foundations.

This transit can be considered a time of "crisis" when actual events are likely to occur. One now has some concrete results from the earlier experiments, and need to form a more stable base of operations following on from the earlier phase of the cycle. So "transplanting" may be necessary. Experiences now may take the form of things like moving house, divorce, marriage, or a new job. In effect "establishing a new home (roots)" – which can mean any area of life over which one has some control. Even a desk in an office. Building new foundations requires giving up relationships and activities that have outlived their usefulness. Symptoms of this are considering home improvements or extensions, or simply moving furniture around. It would be well to consider what is the real need.

Think of a plant being moved from its pot in the greenhouse into the garden.

Results now are those achieved inwardly rather than outwardly, so it may be that no actual event occurs. In fact there may be the sense that one's experiments have resulted in defeat. There may be numerous reasons for this, perhaps based upon being unable to discover the right "market" in the previous stage. One's ideas may be "ahead of their time". It may be one's karma. However, if one has acted positively from the beginning of the cycle there will be a sense of growing self-confidence, which may be the real reason for the experiences offered. There is a sense of power from settling one's inner doubts about what may or may not work.

One is becoming "The Master of one's Own House". New attitudes are established. A new routine and way of life. A new Purpose.

THE CYCLE OF GROWTH STAGE 4 (TRANSPLANTING)

We now have psychological development as the next step towards becoming an individual. The child recognises the difference between inner and outer life, and forms a "persona" ("mask" , or "shell") as a defence against the outside world into which it is about to enter. This refers to 4 to 7 years of age when the child is beginning to associate with people outside the home. This is the "Oedipus/Elektra Age" when the child flirts with the parent of the opposite sex and is rejected – so needing to find the "other" outside the family.

5th. HOUSE TRANSIT – POWER. SELF EXPRESSION. CREATIVITY

Leo : The Lion. Fixed (Controlled) Fire. Power. "All the world is a stage".

Growth from stable roots. Controlling others. Self-confidence. Centre of activity. Personal domain. Action from love of the activity rather than material rewards. Hobbies. Sports. Caring for "children". Creativity from within one's self rather than trying to affect society.

If all has gone well so far in the cycle there will be a renewed sense of power and purpose to life. An increased self-confidence. Perhaps a sense of "promotion" from having direct, personal control of some area of life. The test is how this power is expressed and used. The necessity is that one acts out the new purpose or activity. If other people are not in accord then go forward alone. The danger is that one may believe the final goal has been achieved. When one demonstrates self-confidence there is less opposition from other people. Those that might challenge us move away, and we may attract weaker people ("children") looking for something or someone to believe in. This can offer a false sense of security because we become surrounded by people who seem to agree with us, and give us our own way. There will always be people for or against us.

Actual events would be related to the establishment of one's self as the centre of a sphere of operation. This could be in the sense of becoming the leader of some group, or family - such as when forming one's own business, starting a family, or taking up some occupation, sport, or hobby that one does for love, rather than gain.

The importance here is what principles we express through our personality rather than allowing the energies to inflate our ego. To become a creative channel. With power comes responsibility. The test is that of overcoming one's own human nature and not allowing this sense of power to be used simply to get one's own way in everything, or to prove the strength of one's ego in a battle of wills. The symptoms of this include such things as a yearning for fame or glamour, a powerful need to beget children, or suspicion of other's motives. Activities that are intended to make a personal mark in the outside world. Such behaviour indicates that one is not fully integrated inwardly, and it is still controlled by external appearances. Seeking outward pleasures and recognition rather than inner development. Leading by power, rather than by example. "Keeping up with the Jones's".

THE CYCLE OF GROWTH STAGE 5 (POWER. CREATIVITY)

This is the beginning of the 3rd. Octave of The Cycle of Growth. Between ages 7 to 12 is a time of psychological "latency", there are no major changes. The child becomes an "actor" playing his or her newly designated role. He or she has developed a persona or "mask" as a reaction to life experiences so far. This can be considered a form of defence, or vehicle, from which to approach a wider experience. Within those limits, or boundaries, the individual is "master of his/her house". This is self-control. The child is in primary school where he is taught to put work before pleasure and judged according to his practical creativity. Art rather than Science.

6th. HOUSE TRANSIT – SERVICE TO SELF. HEALTH

Cycle of Growth Stage 6 (Service to Self. Health).

(Virgo. The Virgin. Mutable Earth. Needs something to become complete.)

Balancing service to self and others. Choice of work. Maintaining personal health. Development. Specialisation. Division of labour. Developing talents.

Experiences during transit of the 6th. House will depend upon how power has been used previously. The basic activity of this period is the refinement and development of one's skills before entering a more public environment. One needs to focus energy and specialise in some field of activity. This is a test of humility in recognising one's failings and need for further development. Although this may suggest a more subservient role, and a return to a more childish state of existence, the difference here is that we consciously choose the subject and teacher. One may also become a teacher. Paradoxically, in serving others we also serve ourselves. They enable us to focus on, and further develop, a particular set of skills.

Negatively, a common scenario occurs when the expansive transit of the 5th. House has been used for egocentric motives, and one's field of control has expanded too far beyond the foundations established during the transit of the 4th. House . Things get out of control. The individual attempts to personally be the centre of all activities of the "kingdom" which grows beyond the capabilities of one person to control. In such a situation one would normally appoint helpers. However, the price of able helpers is a share of the power, which includes being able to make decisions without having to seek the prior agreement of the "King" or "Queen" each time. If one has attracted "yes-men" and flatterers, who by definition are weak, they will fade away, or be of no use when help is really needed. In this scenario the result is often ill health from overwork, when the physical body or mind can no longer take the strain. The result is often a symbolic, and real, "heart attack". Misuse of power at that time could result in authority being removed altogether and the acceptance of a position in life with little or no opportunity for decision-making.

An example of this is that a strong Leo influence tends to bring a drive to form one's own business. Fire people are not too good at dealing with the detailed "nitty gritty", so the first helper they usually need is an accountant.

Although there is generally an increased workload as a result of the 5th. House period of expansion, we can also see a possible ego-centric motive for overwork - "I am the only one who can do the job properly" . Unrealistic pride.

We must also not lose sight of the fact that many people are destined for a lone path at this time, when the test is to not become over-burdened by taking on too many responsibilities or accept other people's tasks unnecessarily. "Service to Others" does have its limitations. This can contain a sense of humility too. One cannot solve everyone's problems. If others are not doing things correctly, they can be trained – and will want to do so. Otherwise we can leave them in the care of karma. Again, this means giving up some of one's power and control – and sense of "knowing what is best".

THE CYCLE OF GROWTH STAGE 6 (PERSONAL SERVICE. HEALTH)

At 12 to 23 years of age the child learns that survival depends upon maintaining physical health and the services one offers to others and varies from person to person. Having been "rejected" at home there is teenage rebellion which is part of a powerful inner drive to discover a new individual path. This is the age of Puberty and finding one's place among one's peers of the same sex, although hormones begin pumping in preparation for the next stage of Partnerships. This is a step forward in establishing an individual, personal identity. Having done so, the next Stage will bring challenges from the opposite sex.

3RD. QUARTER - AUTUMN

7th. HOUSE TRANSIT – FLOWERING. SOCIAL ADVANCE. PARTNERSHIP

Cycle of Growth Stage 7 (Partners. "Friends and Enemies").

Libra : The Scales. Cardinal Air. Balance. Adjustment. Seeking a mate.

New partnerships. Seeking common goals. Step forward into more public role. Social service

With the transit of a planet through the 7th. House we reach another "Crisis Point" of Change. We are half way through the cycle of the Houses of the Birth Chart. The focus at this time is on one to one relationships, and beginning to make a bigger contribution to the society in which one lives. Personal development so far has been in the more private areas of life behind the scenes. Further growth requires the acceptance of a more public role in a wider sphere of activity. Here one has even less control over the environment and therefore needs to have a more flexible approach.

One comes into contact with people who can provide support (or challenge) the next stage of the process. The first step away from the past "home" towards a broader, more public, lifestyle. This could mean divorce and/or marriage, but the scope also includes business partners and other relationships. It could mean accepting an occupation that involves more responsibility for offering some service to others. So job changes are likely – perhaps as a result of the training received during the 6th. House transit. It also includes "enemies" – people who seem to obstruct our progress – but could give a more objective viewpoint.

Results also indicate that this can also mean that the subject is affected by changes in the life of a close partner – such as from his or her illness or redundancy.

Much depends upon the age of the subject when this transit occurs. During childhood this will be mainly under the control of parents. Later on the goal is still largely unconscious, more related to reproducing (or escaping from) the circumstances of the traditional parental home during early life and establishing one's own separate place in the world. The creative function related to that of producing children. It is worth noting here the extreme power of the inner, psychological, forces that are exerted. If this were not the case we would probably all still be living with our parents.

One of the problems is that if there is an existing relationship, it will need to adapt to the new circumstances or die. There needs to be some common goal that transcends the personalities of both parties. It could mean that our existing partner can accept a different role. Unfortunately in today's society the "call" is often misheard or misinterpreted. In the face of the prospect of an uncertain future, the need for new growth is translated into the biological terms of past experience. If there is a change of partnership it is often an attempt to regain the blissful ignorance of the past (" a newer model"). Sex is a powerful magnet.

The 7th. House is opposite the 1st. House (Seed). Here we have to remember that if the seed is to fulfil its destiny it must eventually reproduce. It cannot achieve this alone. Nature produces new Seeds in preparation for the next cycle.

THE CYCLE OF GROWTH STAGE 7 (PARTNERS)

At age 23 we begin an adult life. Having established a personal identity based on our life experiences so far, the inner, unconscious, world needs to rebalance. In simplest terms this can be that between Masculine and Feminine energies. Astrology shows that there is no difference between the Birth Charts of a man or woman born at the same time and place. The inner drive to Wholeness (Health. Holiness) leads us to experiment with our "opposites" ("Friends and Enemies") to find and release the energies that have been suppressed or repressed to enable our social survival so far. These "missing parts" are projected on to other people who seem to possess them to bring them to our conscious attention.

8th. HOUSE TRANSIT – INTERCOURSE. TEAM EFFORTS. SHARED RESOURCES.

Cycle of Growth Stage 8 (Sex. Intercourse. Death).

(Scorpio : The Scorpion, Eagle, or Dove. Fixed Water. Sex. Death & Regeneration. The selfish ego must 'die' to fulfil its needs for relationship with others)

Sharing. Teamwork. Adapting to the needs of others. Synergy. Courtship. Cross-pollination. Sex.

Scorpio has 3 different symbols depending on where the focus of motivation lies, and is ultimately concerned with the transcendence of the material world – especially after death. This is also symbolised by the transformation of a caterpillar into a butterfly. We can see that one can be in any state at any particular time.

1. The Scorpion/Serpent (Caterpillar) is the lowest level where one's attention is on sex and selfish earthly pursuits.
2. The Eagle (Chrysalis. "Shell") where one has control over the emotions and is able to remain objectively still in the flow of life around. At this level is the possibility of manipulating others without seeming to take any action. One still expects something in return for one's efforts.
3. The Dove (Butterfly) where one is focused on more humanitarian pursuits and group ideals.

Plants produce flowers, sweets and perfume to help them reproduce. So does the human world.

Traditionally this is the House of "Sex and Death". Although life events now can be quite literal in meaning – there is the possibility of coming into contact with death as a reminder of our impermanent existence on Earth - we can nowadays offer a wider interpretation. The "Death" is actually that of the untamed, selfish ego that needs to co-operate with others in order to survive. The past must die to make room for new life.

The 8th. House of one's Birth Chart is concerned with "shared resources", and is opposite the 2nd. House which is concerned with "personal resources". Now we are concerned with the lesson that there is always some sort of price to pay for co-operation - not always money - and the fact that we can achieve more from teamwork than acting alone – to mutual benefit. Synergy is where the whole becomes more than the sum of its parts. However, some form of sacrifice is necessary.

The simplest level is that of normal commercial interchange. The lesson that we have to give something to get something back. Consider how far mankind has evolved from the need for each of us to make or grow or barter goods to survive. Such things as science and technology and other intellectual pursuits would not exist today ("they neither sow nor reap"). The House is also concerned with taxes and inheritances. The joint resources of a Family, Society, or Country. So there is also the possibility of being involved in legal activities and disputes during this transit – especially those concerned with wills, inheritances, and divorce settlements. Private events can become public knowledge.

Another level it is concerned with sexual intercourse that produces children. At another, the division of labour such as where one partner works to earn money while the other takes care of the home. A division that has become a little blurred and complicated nowadays. The principle is based on each individual using their specialised abilities on behalf of the whole. Rather like a football team that has a goalkeeper, and various attackers and defenders. Each contributing to the "goal" in their own way. The main point being that the goal is an achievement of something that transcends individual or personal achievement. All participants share the results. Each being enabled to develop their special skill further. The price is that we have to give up part of our selfhood, and some of our selfish desires, to achieve something bigger.

When a planet transits the 8th. House such matters need to receive the focus of our attention. The primary need is to keep focused on one's goals in the face of difficulties or distractions that arise – especially that of maintaining or achieving a stable economic and financial base. It may be a time where the care of children is required – certainly an additional expense, and a requirement to apportion responsibilities for care. There may be financial or taxation problems. There may be a need to get out of debt or otherwise stabilise finances. On another level we may need to obtain funding or support for a venture that has been developing "behind the scenes" of life and is becoming ready to be launched on a wider basis. Another kind of "baby". Sometimes it is just practical help, or moral support that is needed rather than money. Perhaps we need to employ a professional helper.

The main aim here is survive the period and end up in a position of physical, financial, and social "health" - having discovered one's real priorities for expenditure of time, money, and effort.

THE CYCLE OF GROWTH STAGE 8 (SEX. DEATH)

On the surface one has experimented with one or more Partners. There is a "call" to discover a more permanent, inner, Individuality.

This Stage begins at age 42 and ends with physical death. The stage is preceded by the beginning of physical deterioration. It is of note that not many people lived until 40 years of age in the not so distant past. The trend is more noticeable in the sporting world by inability to compete with younger people. This is also the time of female menopause.

In this modern world, with an age expectancy of 100 years it will be longer than the whole of the previous life. This is the time of the Jungian "Mid Life Crisis" which brings opportunity to develop one's self beyond what has been conditioned by society so far and discover a truer, inner, Centre. 42 years is the mid-point of the 84 year cycle of Uranus which has been developing since birth. At this "Full Moon" time there is some sort of "vision" of what this new Centre might be. What follows is a matter of individual Will to overcome the social conditioning so far. The main symptom is an inner discontent, or boredom, despite having an outwardly successful life. Most people may not hear the call, or, if they do, ignore it in favour of social acceptance - when there is an attempt to rediscover past satisfaction with such things as a new baby ("before it is too late") a new house, a new car, or a new partner.

9th. HOUSE TRANSIT – CONCEPTION. CONCEPTS. BROADENING THE MIND

(Sagittarius : The Archer. Mutable Fire. Conception. Mental conception. Seeking beyond one's-self to find greater meaning. Life after "death")

Mind broadening. Study. Travel. Religion. Broader social viewpoint. Foreign influences. "In laws". Law.

The 9th. house is traditionally that of "higher learning" such as schools and universities.

It is possible that the previous 8th.House "Sex and Death" experience now leads us to explore possibilities of life after 'death'. Sexual reproduction to produce children is one way of achieving this at a genetic level. What else one leaves behind in passing is another way. This is also a time that may require attention to legal matters, especially those concerned with taxes, wills and inheritances. Perhaps a wider view of how disputes can be settled. Becoming acquainted with the wider, impersonal, laws of our existence.

One of the traditional concerns of the 9th. House that is often missed by modern astrologers is "in laws". This is quite important when we consider it as part of the cycle. In general terms, having come into partnership in some way, such as by marriage, we begin to meet people who they know, and we have not yet met. They have a life and activities outside the partnership. Such activities are often outside the scope of our personal experience. They are "foreign" to us. This takes on more meaning when we consider the more universally accepted concerns of the 9th House. Which are related to "long distance travel". It is natural that we be invited to share in these "alien" activities, and thus broaden our experience.

A more modern association with the 9th.House is that of Conception. This can relate to our own physical conception, or mental conception. The symbolism of each House has a natural relationship with that of a Sign, in this case the 9th. Sign Sagittarius. In the annual cycle this is the preparation for the Christmas and New Year period. The promise of Rebirth.

We need to make special note here that our journey of life begins at Conception, the experiences of the later weeks we spend in the womb being as significant as any other. Perhaps they could be more important than we realise. Exploration of this area of knowledge has, in the past, been limited to times when things go wrong. As with other areas nowadays, new technology is opening up new possibilities for exploration.

Although travel or moving house is likely around the time of this transit we must not lose sight of the fact that its purpose in terms of the cycle is to broaden our mind and outlook for future possibilities, as well as gain a broader understanding of the laws that govern Nature, Society, or the Universe in general.

This brings us to other concerns of the 9th. House, which are directly related to broadening of the mind. Abstract knowledge - outside personal experience. This is the natural domain of schools and universities, churches, or other areas where training and education takes place. It is unlikely that earlier life experience gives all the knowledge needed to fulfil our purpose - so we often decide that some sort of training or study is important at this time. Important subjects are those that relate to understanding ourselves in relationship to the rest of humanity such as Law, Religion, Philosophy, Psychology and Astrology. Unfortunately, for many, there is an irrational fear of exploring such areas. In any such situation it is a help to realise that thousands of people are involved in such areas on a daily basis. This transit brings the lesson of needing to remove the prejudice and fear that blinds us to the broader realities of life. To put the traditions of our birth into a wider perspective. "Know Thyself". An example is the new evidence arising from the study of Evolution and DNA being challenged by established religions which will need to expand their horizons – exploring the Spirit, rather than the Letter, of the Law.

THE CYCLE OF GROWTH STAGE 9 (CONCEPTION)

This Stage is the beginning of the 1st. Octave of The Cycle of Growth.

Apart from our conception prior to birth at the beginning of the 1st. Octave, which covers our life in the womb, this is also the beginning of "The Transcendent Octave" concerned with more academic or theoretical concepts outside our normal life experience. We can seek new "foreign" mental concepts by studying subjects which are "taboo" in normal society.

4TH. QUARTER : WINTER

10th. HOUSE TRANSIT – PEAK OF ACHIEVEMENT. HARVEST

(Capricorn : The Mountain Goat. Cardinal Earth. Climbing the material "ladder of success". Higher aims. New Year Resolutions)

Harvesting fruits of past efforts for good or ill. Promotion. Responsibility. Duty. Prestige. Limelight.

Transit of the 10th House is probably the one that is most easily remembered, and therefore most useful for checking that the birth time is correct - especially by observing the Personal Transit of Saturn. This is because one now reaps the harvest of all one's efforts throughout the cycle. Whereas previous activity has tended to be in the background of life, the fruits of one's labour are now in concrete form and evident for all to see. For good or ill. One's popularity and social standing, or otherwise, is at its highest. If nothing significant was noticed during the 1st. House transit it now may be possible to look back at that time to see how everything started.

We see examples of this in our external world when individual "stars" come to public attention and seem to be continually in the news (for better or worse) and later seem to fade away.

Since the 1st. House transit one has learned how to fit one's personal aims in with those of others. The task now is to take some public or professional stand in full public view as a result. One reaches a position of power and responsibility RELATED TO ONE'S PAST EFFORTS. This can mean things like job promotion, or invitations to join governing bodies of organisations. Perhaps teaching or otherwise reporting on one's activities. This can also mean social ostracism as a result of attempting to be too independent, separating oneself from society, or being involved in anti-social activities. In the School of Life bad examples or mistakes can be as useful as good.

It is important that one now focuses on the job at hand. This will probably mean taking on added responsibilities, and therefore time for other activities will be limited. This is a time of consolidation rather than further expansion. The period of transit is limited and will be followed by a "Winter" decline in preparation for the new cycle which starts when the planet eventually transits the 1st. House once again. It is also important that one does not allow one's integrity to be compromised. A strong moral stance must be maintained. We have only to observe the media to realise that, when coming to public view, much can be revealed that we would rather have kept hidden. It also arouses jealousy and other negative emotions in some people, who do not understand the hard work that has been put into achieving the position, and we become attacked by them.

A danger at this time is that we may let success "go to our head" and push aside new "Conceptions", ideas for future growth. "Killing our brain-children". At least "bear" in mind that this experience is temporary. We can now see the symbolic relationship of the meaning of this time to the story of the biblical "Virgin Birth" which contains more than reference to normal human reproduction. The 10th House relates to the sign of Capricorn with its symbolism of rebirth at Christmas and the Winter Solstice. Extending the symbolism, human conception requires that just a single sperm fertilises the egg. Once one penetrates, defences are put up so others are rejected.

In terms of a Birth Chart this is the House wherein the mother first becomes aware of her pregnancy and the possible birth to come. Perhaps this is really when our life ambitions are set, positive or negative, from her attitude to the coming new life . At least until we find our own life pathway.

I have noticed that female subjects are likely to bear a child around this time. Usually their first.

The 10th House of Career is opposite the 4th. House of Home and Roots. The conflict between the two areas is a common life experience. One usually has to be neglected in favour of the other. Therefore the draw towards the Home can be very powerful at this time as a form of compensation. At its peak the planet in question has begun its return to the 4th. House.

THE CYCLE OF GROWTH STAGE 10 (HARVEST. PEAK)

The 10th. House refers to the time of Christmas and the rebirth of The SUN at the Winter Solstice which has been celebrated for millennia. It is also the time celebrating the birth of Jesus as the SON. The symbolism refers to the "birth" of new concepts and ideas. "New Year Resolutions". The continuance of the story appears in many symbolic forms with the same meaning. In the Bible with Moses and Jesus the "old king" hears of the birth of the child as a possible "new king" and feels challenged by the news. He therefore orders the death of all new born children (who somehow manage to escape, to reappear later on). In human life, the father realises that he will no longer have his wife's sole attention.

In external symbolism we have ceremonies relating to the "death" of the old year and "birth" of the new – which does not appear in physical form until Spring.

In terms of human development this is the time after conception that the mother becomes aware of her pregnancy and begins to tell others. Research by psychologists have shown that our life in the womb affects us after birth. From this time until the actual birth the experiences of the mother as she reacts to her environment are passed on to the foetus.

At another level, this is symbolic of the historical reaction of Society (especially the Church) in attempting to suppress the development of new ideas. So we see inner and outer attempts to suppress our search for new knowledge.

11th. HOUSE TRANSIT – DISSATISFACTION. INVENTION.

(Aquarius : The Water Carrier. Fixed Air. Communication. Invention. Change. Independence. Rebellion.)

Social decline. Re-assess aims. Challenging outmoded ideas & traditions. Inventing new.

Having achieved social position and prestige in the 10th House we could assume that we would be satisfied with the current situation. However, to arrive at this destination we have had to focus energies on achieving the goal over a considerable period of time. Not only has this required that we ignore interesting side issues that may have arisen, but we also have had to adapt our original aims to fit in with the social climate. So at this time, apart from positive and negative responses from those around, we have a personal mixture of feelings of success and failure.

If successful, we may attempt to prolong the situation for as long as possible. However this is often counteracted by an inner sense of being a 'slave' to one's position or office. There is a sense of "noblesse oblige", and maintaining one's position takes continual effort. In the midst of success one is at everyone's beck and call. Privacy becomes limited. One becomes surrounded by people who, apart from flattery, take more than they give. To appear in public makes one vulnerable to attack from all and sundry with their own agendas to carry out, or who do not realise the considerable effort required to achieve the position. Perhaps one's health begins to suffer, or perhaps a sense of boredom sets in. One's inner emotional energy becomes drained.

If failures outweigh successes at this time, there is the likelihood that one might attempt to stir up trouble in revenge. Blaming other people or society for one's own failure. Perhaps joining groups involved in anti-social behaviour. This is a futile waste of time and energy because we gradually stir up increasing opposition and become hopelessly outnumbered. While fighting against, rather than for, something we can lose sight of possibilities for positive growth.

There is, however, a middle path where one may be called upon to use one's public position to openly challenge outmoded or unfair forms of tradition or government. Perhaps joining a group of people dedicated to such a purpose – or undertaking some form of self-development. We often see "celebrities" offering support to charitable organisations during this period. Law, Tradition, Order, Routine, and Habit are necessary to our survival, so we need to replace bad structures with good one's rather than trying to eradicate them altogether. That would lead to anarchy.

Another manifestation we see frequently is when celebrities seem to give up their chosen career to become a host in television quiz or chat shows, or similar. Only the results of time will tell if this is a positive or negative activity. Have they lost their way, or sense of purpose, or got lazy? If new seeds are sown at the proper time later on then it would seem to be opportunity for growth to continue. We must also note that, because the 11th. House is opposite the 5th. House, similar ego issues can appear here too.

Eventually, whatever the situation, the cycles of life continue to draw us forward to further new experience. This could also be forced by actual events. In this modern age there is no such thing as a "job for life". Redundancy is a possibility during this transit. Now is an opportunity to look at one's original aims and see if there is something that can be revived or improved upon. Nowadays new technology is advancing very quickly – perhaps new and better tools are available. Perhaps one invents the tools that can help build a new future. Greater freedom.

Again, we see this time demonstrated in the lives of famous people when they have been in public view for a period and later fade into the background.

CYCLE OF GROWTH STAGE 11 (DISCONTENT)

In the Biblical story of the birth of Jesus his parents ran away to avoid letting him be killed.

The Stage has dual planetary rulerships which symbolise the choice of this time.

As we have seen Saturn rules the 10th.House. Saturn is symbolic of a structured material life and rules large organisations of people such as big business, government, and church. Traditionally Saturn rules this Stage as well. Saturn is the furthest planet that is visible with the unaided eye.

When Uranus was discovered it was given dual rulership of Aquarius and the 11th. House. Its basic symbolism is related to Science and Technology, and the inventions of the modern world which are bringing a faster rate of Change nowadays. Its discovery was the result of new technology.

The inner individual struggle of this Stage is symbolised by that between Saturn (Government. Tradition) and Uranus (The Individual). During The Aquarian Age (ruled by Uranus) it is demonstrated by the rebellion of the population against unfair oppression by authority and slogans such as "a fair day's work for a fair day's pay" and "no taxation without representation". Opportunities for individuals to have more control over their destiny. Even today we see rebellions against dictatorship. Inwardly, at a personal level, Uranus is symbolic of the Jungian "process of Individuation" that takes us outside material social rules and laws into a more universal experience.

It is a matter of personal Will whether Saturn or Uranus rules this stage.

12th. HOUSE TRANSIT – WITHDRAWAL. CONFINEMENT. DECAY

(Pisces : The Fishes. Sacrifice the past to move forward. The Collective Unconscious rules everything).

Each of the Houses relating to Water Signs carries the necessity to give up the past to make way for a broader future. Here we have Confinement awaiting birth/new cycle. Clearing of past. Settling debts. Rewards or penalties. Karma.

In relationship to the Birth Chart this is the time of confinement when the mother has to reduce physical activity and retire into the home in preparation for the birth, which is the concern of the following 1st.House transit.

In Nature it is late Winter - nearly Spring. Seeds are in the ground waiting for the right time to germinate. The waste products of the past have been converted into fertiliser for future growth. The ground prepared for new growth. Death has made space for new life. Even if one is still carrying out normal daily tasks there is a sense of isolation. This is a time of transition.

Although one can be receiving rewards for past services, the task now is one of self-analysis. The planet has gone full cycle and one has had concrete results from one's efforts. Before one can begin a new one there is a need to re-evaluate one's successes and failures - especially in the light of one's original aims at the beginning of the cycle. Destroying the "weeds" and making space for "new crops" to grow.

This is a time of Withdrawal and working on matters inwardly rather than outwardly. The external world needs to become less focused. There may be participation in artistic, religious, musical, or other non-practical activities like entertainment and travel to aid this process. Taking holidays, or spiritual retreat. Perhaps taking courses or joining groups involved in some form of self-development - such as religion, psychology, meditation, Astrology, or Yoga. Perhaps, finally, completing tasks that have been left undone. Or simply resting.

This is often a time of "trial separation" of married couples in consideration that "something has to change".

Attempts to ignore this requirement could result in being forced into "retirement" from external activities by illness or some other form of "imprisonment". This House traditionally rules Prisons, Hospitals, Monasteries, Convents and other areas of personal isolation as well as "underground" structures such as sewerage and drainage. Even God rested after the Creation.

This is a time of repayment of debts – to one's self and others. Giving and receiving forgiveness. Sometimes it is easier to forgive others than one's self. We can see positive reasons for allowing one's self to "forget it" now. The task is to enter into the next cycle free of "baggage" from the past. One will try to "do better next time".

One now realises that the interminable process of life is more important than one's practical achievements, which are "transit-ory". Another danger at this time is that of becoming self-satisfied with one's achievements and assuming that this is the end to one's struggle in life. There is a need to realise that all structures require regular maintenance. The body and mind need exercise, otherwise they collapse. Prepare for the new "Spring".

The 12th. House is opposite the 6th. House which is concerned with one's health and physical well-being. If we have neglected maintenance to our homes or other possessions – especially the physical body – this would be the time to have problems forcing them to our attention.

Despite the physical symptoms, accidents or health problems at this time are more likely to have psychosomatic than physical causes. We can see how seeming negatives of ill health, and even abuse of alcohol and drugs (also traditional concerns of this House) can actually assist the 12th. House "forgetting" process. Indeed, some form of exploration in the field of Psychology may be especially beneficial at this time.

At another level, this is the "House of Karma" where debts are repaid for good or ill. "As You Give, So Shall You Receive". The final harvest and judgement of our past actions before a new phase of life. At the end of a cycle everything must balance to Zero.

CYCLE OF GROWTH STAGE 12 (WITHDRAWAL. CONFINEMENT)

The 12th. House and Sign also have a dual planetary rulership – that of Jupiter and Neptune. Which planet rules this Stage is decided by whether Saturn (Tradition. Society) overcomes Uranus (Individuality) in the previous Stage.

Jupiter is the traditional ruler with the principle of "Expansion". With no reaction to new influences at Cycle of Growth Stage 11 (Discontent) we expand our experience of past activities. There is no change.

Symbolically, Neptune is active just before Spring to break down the remains of the previous year's growth to fertilise that of the coming year. If Uranus overcomes Saturn at Cycle of Growth Stage 11, then Neptune acts to dissolve the remains of our psychological blocks so we can enter a new life.

The symbolism relates to the time that Jesus spent "in the wilderness" when he was tempted by the Devil to use his powers to gain material or social status rather than face crucifixion. His crucifixion and rebirth is celebrated at each year at Easter Time which occurs at Cycle of Growth Stage 1 (Seed) – the beginning of Spring and new life on Earth. Jesus became the "seed" of the Christian Church. His Resurrection is symbolic of the rebirth at Spring.

SATURN – PERSONAL TRANSITS

Although the focus of this book is on using Generic Astrology without having a Birth Chart, it is so easy to get a free Birth Chart on line nowadays that it is worthwhile considering the Personal Saturn Cycle because :-

1. *The "crisis" events of the Personal Saturn Cycle tend to be more notable because of the longer timescale. It is often possible – with other factors - to use them to correct a Birth Chart where the birth time is inaccurate or unknown.*
2. *Despite adding another complication to a narrative meant to be simplified, it does serve as a contrast to show the difference between Generic and Personal Transits. That is, where the Individual fits in with the norm.*
3. *We are even more free of the complications brought by the planets that have shorter cycles.*

We look at Lady Diana Spencer's life in this context at the end of the chapter.

THE BIRTH CHART

For this task it is necessary to have an accurate Birth Chart. You will need the Date and Place of birth as well as a birth time accurate to within 2 hours. The latter is because the earth has a 24 hour rotation so there is a new Ascendant, or Rising Sign every 2 hours. This is the cusp of the 1st. House which, as we have seen in the [BIRTH CHART HOUSES] chapter, is used to provide the basis of a Birth Chart at a personal level.

For the purpose of this chapter, we are only interested in the position of Saturn by House.

Once you have a Birth Chart I suggest that you :-

1. Check the House that Saturn is in.
2. Refer to the Generic Life Diary form and put the House number against the year of birth, the use the highlighted numbers in the Saturn column to add 3 houses each time.
3. Mark the years when transits of the 1st., 4th., 7th. and 10th. Houses occur. Because Saturn moves slowly a year either way makes no real difference.

JUPITER AND SATURN

JUPITER

*** The glyph of Jupiter consists of the Semi-Circle of Soul combined with the Cross of Matter.**

*** It shows how the higher mind can create abstract concepts beyond the limitations of physical constraint. Or *Illusion*.**

*** Its principle is Expansion.**

To understand the effects of Jupiter and Saturn it is helpful to consider them as a pair because their natures are in opposition to one another. We have to note that, in themselves, the planets have no effect on us. They are only indicators of deeper universal forces, or archetypal principles, that we and they are subject to. They can be considered to be like twigs dropped into a river where they show the directions of otherwise invisible currents.

We can see that their glyphs, or symbols, are the same one drawn at different angles.

In some way, in the conflict between the 2 planets we can see a depiction of that between God (Expansion. Growth) and The Devil (Materiality).

The main principles behind Jupiter are Expansion, and Growth. It rules the Sign of Sagittarius which is the Mutable (changeable) Fire Sign. Apart from natural growth processes, Jupiter/Sagittarius is concerned with such areas as social interaction and academic study where we learn from other people without having had practical experience ourselves. Such as from books. So Churches, Schools, and Universities come under this heading. Foreign Travel is also included as a form of Mind Broadening experience.

Without Jupiter nothing would grow. There would be stagnation and death. We currently have a good example of a negative Jupiter/Sagittarius. Pluto, with its eccentric orbit cycle of 248 years is in the same Sign for many years, and so affects whole generations of people in the same way. As I write this, it has just finished transiting Sagittarius where it produced religious extremism and terrorism – all in the name of abstract idealism. Theories and beliefs without factual evidence. An inability to recognise that we all worship One God and it is just the outer form (Saturn/Capricorn) that is different.

PERSONAL JUPITER

The position of Jupiter in a Birth Chart by House, Sign, and aspects shows how we can best use Jupiter energy to produce Growth in our lives. Those with Sun Sign Sagittarius are learning how to generate and use the energy. The House position of Jupiter shows where it is most naturally used.

SATURN

* **The components of the glyph of Saturn are the same as those of Jupiter. Here the Cross of Matter rises above the Semi-Circle of Soul.**
* **The abstract concepts of expansive Jupiter are forced into practical use - demanding physical evidence.**
* **The principle of Saturn is Consolidation.**

The main principles of Saturn/Satan and its associated Sign, Capricorn, are concerned with Consolidation and practical organisation and stability. At a social level its principle is exemplified by the laws that rule society – such as those found in Government and large business organisations that require fixed rules. We see the negative effect of Saturn when people and organisations get too entrenched, or fixed, in their rules and habits that they find it impossible to change – especially in the face of new discoveries and the increased rate of (external) change nowadays. History shows many blocks to progress by Religions and Governments. As I write this, Pluto is entering the Sign of Capricorn where there is demonstration of the modifying effect of the Sign on Jupiter from increased security and laws against terrorism. Even normal members of the population are having to accept some restriction on their activities – especially where Jupiter/Sagittarius foreign travel is concerned.

At a basic level Saturn governs our incarnation into a physical body – with all its limitations and needs. Traditionally he is also "The Lord of Karma", which, apart from the kind of physical existence we inherit at birth, is concerned with "as you sow, so shall you reap" – which can be interpreted at an Agricultural level as well as the archetypal connection of Saturn/Capricorn with Cycle of Growth Stage 10 (Peak. Harvest).

PERSONAL SATURN

At a personal level, Saturn can be viewed as the Habits of living we set up, or, more consciously, Self-Discipline that can focus the Sun Sign energies to achieve a practical goal – perhaps over a long period of time. (Think in terms of its 30 year cycle). We do this by using Will and a certain ruthlessness in cutting out side issues - or other activities that could waste time, energy, or money which could be used in pursuit of the goal.

A main example of this focus of energy is that of a Career when someone can start as a floor sweeper and, after many years, rise through the ranks to become Chairman of the Board. Or a similar career in the military.

We note that the "I Ching", or Chinese "Book of Changes" (Hexagram 60), states that "THERE MUST BE LIMITATION - EVEN TO LIMITATION".

Those with Sun in Capricorn, or with a strongly placed Saturn in their Birth Chart, are learning this life lesson. In effect, there is less Free Will and a need to balance the demands of what Inner Saturn wants, as shown in the Birth Chart, with External Saturn as the traditions, rules and habits of Society.

Apart from the House position, the focus of our Saturn activities in life is basically defined by the Element of the Sign that the planet is in when we are born. Its tendency is to amplify the negative effects of the Element (or is this a result of past lives ?).

- SATURN IN EARTH (Taurus, Virgo, Capricorn) is concerned with controlling down-to-earth practical matters and care of the human body – such as by having fixed routines in business organisation and management. As we have seen, Saturn is very compatible with the Earth element because it likes practical, material, goals. A practical career.
- SATURN IN AIR (Gemini, Libra, Aquarius) is concerned with control of the Mind and Thinking processes. There can be too much mental activity. At this level ideas must work in actual practice. This is the area of Science and Experiment. Saturn is compatible with the Air Element where it applies to Logic, Reasoning, and accurate Communication. There may be a speech impediment when young.
- SATURN IN WATER (Cancer, Scorpio, Pisces) is concerned with Feelings and emotional control. This is the area of Art and caring for one's self and others. It brings emotional sensitivity. Saturn is not very compatible with the Water Element where isolation from others can lead to loss of contact with earthy reality.
- SATURN IN FIRE (Aries, Leo, Sagittarius) is concerned with Intuition and control of our basic life energy. There is a tendency to overwork and ignore basic bodily needs, leading to ill health which is often based on heart and blood problems. At a practical level this could mean having power over others and learning to use it. Sharing power by supporting their learning processes rather than trying to control everything. This applies to such fields as having one's own business, Sport, and Entertainment where energies are used to encourage, inspire and motivate. "The rules of the game". Sagittarius is concerned with broadening the mind.

In common with the archetypal nature of the Zodiac Signs, the above lessons can be applied to any planet's elementary position – especially the Sun. With the Moon, we have already learned the lessons of its element position and can tend to rely on it in times of difficulty.

TRANSITING SATURN

Having "set the scene" we summarise that :-

1. THE MOST IMPORTANT POINT IS THAT THE FOCUS OF MEANING AND REQUIRED ACTIVIVITY OF A PERSONAL HOUSE TRANSIT IS IDENTICAL TO THAT ALREADY DESCRIBED FOR THE 12

STAGES OF "THE CYCLE OF GROWTH" RELATED TO JUPITER. THE DIFFERENCE IS THAT JUPITER'S STAGES LAST 1 YEAR AND SATURN'S 2 ½ YEARS.

2. We could equally use any other planet. For example the annual cycle of the Sun (with Mercury and Venus – which are never far away) where each Stage would last 1 month.
3. At a Personal level, Saturn's activity focuses on the Houses of a Birth Chart.
4. Saturn's 30 year orbit means that it is in a House for about 2 ½ years – which varies somewhat because at times it seems to go backwards ("Retrograde") and forwards ("Direct") through the Signs. Retrograde suggests that Saturn has already reached a position in The Zodiac and is going backwards to "reassess" the earlier situation before going forward again.
5. We do not generally get opportunity to use any planet in a Personal way until it first transits the 1st. House of our Birth Chart. Until then the energy is under the control of heredity, parental figures, or other life circumstances. So the position of Saturn in our Birth Chart would tend to show their wishes. Reincarnation suggests that there would be some spiritual purpose for our birth into such early conditioning. That is, not being given much choice early on in life.
6. One of Saturn's many physical manifestations in life takes the form of "Old People" – often referring to grandparental control rather than that of parents. It is from them that comes the early criticism of our actions that shapes the rest of our life. It is a good exercise to recall and reconsider the validity of negative criticisms (or just neutral lack of encouragement, or isolation) we received in childhood related to the personal Elemental lessons mentioned above. Psychologists tend to make their living by doing just that.
7. Among other things, Saturn includes "The fear of making mistakes" (or, rather, the expected social consequences). It is good to recognise that some businesses spend millions of pounds in order to make mistakes – where it is called "Research".
8. In its cycle Saturn has a Generic position in relation to its Stage 1 (Seed) position in the Birth Chart, and a Personal position in relation to its transits through the Houses of the birth chart at one and the same time. We are always subject to Generic Saturn in the form of social traditions, rules, and laws.
9. In Generic terms, which are more concerned with our position in the Society in which we live, we do not generally have control of Saturn until age 30 – which is the end of its first cycle. The suggestion is that we have hopefully achieved the position defined by our Birth Chart and are now in a position to make an informed choice for future activity. We note that it was not until relatively recently that a human lifetime lasted more than 30 years, and that physical deterioration is felt soon after this time – exemplified by the inability of sportspeople to compete with those younger than themselves, and the onset of menopause in women.
10. Personal Saturn requires us to develop the will to achieve personal aims in accordance or conflict with that situation. People with Saturn in the 1st.House of their Birth Charts get strong exterior controls from early childhood. They are "born old".
11. If we do not internally discipline ourselves we will be externally disciplined by others. It is a fact that young children and animals test where the "line is drawn" between. If they do not get clearly defined boundaries there is a strong sense of anxiety from having to make choices they are not equipped for. Lack of parental control usually means that the police get the problem. Some years ago young offenders were given a "short, sharp shock" of military-like discipline. The experiment ceased when authorities found that they were enjoying the experience. At another level, there is a certain comfort in being able to blame someone telling us what to do for (inevitable) mistakes rather than accept responsibility.
12. Saturn is a form of Responsibility. During life we need to decide what responsibilities we accept or deny. It is often arrogant and non-productive to always be "our brother's keeper" rather than let him or her learn for them self.

13. A main purpose of Saturn is TO FOCUS ENERGY on a particular task or goal. As it transits through the Houses and Signs the focus changes to what is required at the time. This is the principle behind Agriculture and "The Cycle of Growth". Generally, to achieve some goal we have to proceed through a sequence of steps in the right order. For example, when building a house it is best to draw up plans first, and then lay the foundations – and so on.

DIANA SPENCER'S PERSONAL SATURN

We cannot know what exactly happened in Diana's private life so I will just consider the crisis points of her Personal Saturn cycle. Because Saturn moves so slowly and her life was short we do not have many of them to consider. However, the ones we have are good examples.

Because Diana was born with Saturn in the 1st. House of her Birth Chart there will not be much difference between her Personal Saturn Cycle or Generic Saturn Cycle. This means 2 things :-

1. She will be tied to a traditional lifestyle and parental values than most of us.
2. Saturn will not transit her Ascendant (1st. House cusp) for the first time (when she would get the opportunity to use Saturn in a personal way) until it has almost completed a full 30 year cycle which emphasises the effect.

When we observe Diana's life we see that this was indeed the case. In fact, being born into the British aristocracy with hundreds of years of family tradition she was more bound by old rules and values than we "normal" people would be. We also see this influence over the rest of her life. She did not escape her family values on leaving home and marrying, as most of us do. In fact, becoming part of the royal family increased her bondage to a strict protocol. In a strange way, almost without taking any personal action, she became instrumental in introducing revolutionary concepts to that staid constitution. We must not under-estimate the power of her Moon in revolutionary Aquarius. Typically, since her death, The Establishment has once again closed ranks and reverted to the previous status quo.

We can use this last fact as a personal example for ourselves in relation to our personal aims and resolutions. It is easy for "revolutionaries" to make a lot of noise and cause temporary upheaval, but to produce lasting effects it is necessary to use the power of Saturn to establish our own Tradition.

In the chapter [ASTROLOGY : CHART EXAMPLES] there is more detailed information about Diana's Birth Chart, in particular her Sun in Cancer and Moon in Aquarius which are of prime importance in defining the main focus of her personal spiritual life lessons.

1961 – CYCLE OF GROWTH STAGE 1 (SEED. BIRTH)

PERSONAL SATURN IN CAPRICORN AND 1ST. HOUSE

With Saturn in its own Sign of Capricorn all the tendencies mentioned will be emphasised.

The effect of Saturn on our early life tends to be from parental, or more usually, grand-parental criticism or control. With a powerful Saturn Birth Chart position there is a tendency to be "born old", when one has to take on greater responsibility than is usually expected of young children. At a simple level, one can be the eldest child in the family and have responsibility to care for brothers and sisters. Some have to actually care for parents who are chronically ill, or at least fend for themselves with little help from family.

A strong Saturn is also an indicator of an "absent father" where the individual, for whatever reason, lacks contact with their father during the early years and therefore lacks experience of the role model. Although he loved her, Earl Spencer tended to be a distant figure in Diana's life.

At a deeper emotional level things are a bit more subtle. Saturn is an indicator of what we were criticised about in our early years. Some area of life where we were expected to be "perfect" – despite being too young to really understand. This will relate to matters concerning the Zodiac Sign of Saturn in the Birth Chart. For example, with Saturn in an Air Sign we will be criticised about such things as our speaking and learning progress – and may even have a speech impediment. It is notable that stuttering is usually a psychological rather than physical problem, and some stutterers sing very well.

In Diana's case, with Saturn in her 1st. House ANY and all of her actions would be criticised. The 1st. House is that which defines our Personal Drive. The things we do for our-self. In the face of such opposition to freedom of action from the powerful "godlike" figures in life the young person retires into submission.

Later on in life the subject exhibits a timid approach to everything from the inner expectation that any personal initiative will be punished – if only verbally. The main problem being that when learning new things we expect to make mistakes – which some parental figures will not tolerate (in others).

In Diana's case, as the first – born, her actual 1st. House birth itself became a "cardinal sin" in that she was not born a boy. She later stated this fact herself. One life aim of the British aristocracy is to produce a son and heir to the family fortunes. Someone to continue uphold and continue the Family Tradition. History shows this to be of prime importance, and a sense of failure of the parents failing to "deliver the goods". For example, this was the reason for Henry VIII's numerous wives. Diana's lack of self-confidence is evident in her outer life.

There is also another subtle effect of false spirituality underlying all this. The aristocracy had a long tradition of "noblesse oblige" where it was expected one used power to help those less fortunate. There is nothing wrong with this on the surface, but to a shy young girl this would have been translated to mean that anything "selfish" was a deadly sin.

Age 6. 1967/8 CYCLE OF GROWTH STAGE 4 (TRANSPLANTING)

Although being under the control of parents during the early years, my experience has shown that their actions have an uncanny reflection in our personal cycles.

Over this time period Diana's mother left the family home and later divorced – something unknown at the time, especially at that social level. Diana was send away from home to boarding school.

Age 15. 1976/7 CYCLE OF GROWTH STAGE 7 (PARTNERS)

The Stage, apart from change in close partnerships, has the effect of bringing us out of life behind the scenes to a more public experience outside the home.

Diana was sent to finishing school in Switzerland, and met Charles for the first time at a social gathering– although she was "too young for him to date".

Age 22. 1983/4 CYCLE OF GROWTH STAGE 10 (HARVEST. PEAK)

The Stage is that of reaping the "harvest" of all one's actions since the original "seed" was sown. One achieves the public position one merits. At a more mundane level this is the Peak time of one's Career. As the Peak time passes there is decline in preparation for planting new "seeds" and starting a new cycle. My experience shows that this is often a likely time for women to give birth – which is entirely in keeping with the symbolic relationship of the Stage to Christmas - with the birth of the SON, and the rebirth of the SUN at the Winter Solstice.

During the intervening period Diana had married Charles and Prince William was born at Stage 10 of her Generic Jupiter Cycle (also, Jupiter was in the 10th. Personal House of her Birth Chart).

During Diana's Career Peak Prince Harry was born, and Charles and Diana had a world tour of official engagements, at some of which Diana was actually representing the Queen. We emphasise that at this time EVERYTHING IS DEPENDANT ON THE ORIGINAL SEED – and we can clearly see that Diana was fulfilling its destiny – albeit according to her family upbringing.

Now follows the decline. Although they continued their official engagements, the relationship between Charles and Diana began to deteriorate. It is interesting to note that Diana's 10th. Career House is ruled by Libra – Sign of Partnerships. Charles brought her to the "peak", and as the relationship declined so did her social position.

We can see that she later experimented with other partnerships – all of which produced different public aspects.

Diana later admitted to 5 suicide attempts during this period, and her bulimia nervosa disorder got worse as she turned her anger against herself (as she had been conditioned to do). We can see this as a prelude to "re-inventing" herself in preparation for a new Stage 1 Seed time.

Age 30. 1991/2 CYCLE OF GROWTH STAGE 1 (SEED)

Generally, the first Saturn Return (to its position in the Birth Chart) is significant because, until that time, we are unconsciously following the "programming" by parents during the early years of life. This can be true even if there is rebellion against it, because there is a tendency to reject "good" as well as "bad". In this context, we note that in the past not many people lived beyond age 30. At this time there is an inner drive to follow our own personal life path. This is similar in meaning to Saturn's transit of our Birth Chart 1st. House which has a more external effect. Diana had Personal Saturn in her 1st. House, so both effects combine.

DIANA AND CHARLES

It is appropriate now to observe the specific traditional conditioning that affected both Diana and Charles because our personal experience will not necessarily be the same. We need to understand the MEANING, or universal "purpose", of this time to relate it to ourselves.

History shows that a prime consideration of people in power is to ensure that their offspring find the right mates to eventually produce heirs to inherit their "kingdoms". In particular, the heir was supposed to be male. At a superficial level this concerns property, and their own particular power base of controlling people. At a deeper archetypal level this relates to the survival of their genes. A prime example in Britain was Henry VIII who found various ways of disposing of his wives until one produced a male heir – something that dominated his whole life.

We have to note that this is not just a personal or individual focus of attention concerned with one's masculine powers. In that realm of Society there is considerable pressure from family and close associates to "perform" because their livelihood depends on it too. Newcomers might introduce unwanted changes. There is an underlying sense of social stigma attached.

In Diana's case we see that there was considerable dismay surrounding her birth because she was female. The Spencers were getting older, and so far had not produced a son. This attitude coloured her early childhood, and she clearly felt "not wanted", stating "I should have been born a boy". I make the point that this is an extreme example of a psychological "life decision" that we all make at an early age "I'm Not OK, You're OK" which comes as a result of our dependency on parents for survival (covered in more detail in my book "The Cycle of Growth").

Charles, as was Henry VIII, was also under pressure to marry. Again, it would have been intense because he was expected to produce a king to succeed himself – bearing in mind that he was 10 years older than Diana. He was 33 years of age when he married Diana in 1981, with his Jupiter transiting its Generic 10th. House (Peak. Harvest. Public View).

In 1991, although Charles and Diana had been living apart for 2 years there now came the OFFICIAL (Saturn) announcement of the separation, instigated by the Queen. They were not actually divorced until their next Crisis Stage(s). We can see that Charles was making his own challenges to The Establishment by relating to Camilla Parker Bowles – who was married at the time. The final divorce in 1996 occurred as Jupiter was transiting its Generic 1st. House (Seed. New Beginnings). He finally married Camilla in 2005 as, in his first one 24 years before, his Generic Jupiter transited its 10th. house (Peak. Harvest. Public View).

We see how single events can be the effect of different Crisis Stages for different people.

Diana now had a public presence of her own and, now making her own decisions, was beginning to work in areas more suited to her Cancer (The Mother) Sun Sign with her concern for disadvantaged children. She became patron to over 100 charities.

The Queen once again intervened and wrote a letter to each asking them to officially end their marriage.

Age 36. 1997/8 CYCLE OF GROWTH STAGE 4 (TRANSPLANTING)

This coincides with her Generic Jupiter Cycle of Growth Stage 1 (Seed) time, and we can see a combination with Saturn in preparation for a “new life”.

The intervening period between the last Stage and this one is that of private planning and re-adjustment. In childhood, Cycle of Growth Stage 4 is the time of forming the “Persona” or mask that we wear to hide our inner feeling and become as actors on “the stage of life”. We can see that Diana selling her dresses for charity and wearing army fatigues in public at this time as symbolic of her new role.

We note that Cycle of Growth Stage 4 has association with Tarot Card VII. The Chariot which was the older equivalent of the modern motor car (progress by control of power). Diana was killed in a car crash.

It seems that Saturn as a powerful influence over her Birth Chart and Life in his role as “Lord of Karma” (and other Harvests) had other goals. Diana died in a tunnel, which is a symbol of transit from one phase of life to another.

ASTROLOGY : CHARTS EXAMPLES

BIRTH CHART FOR : LADY DIANA SPENCER

BORN : 1st July 1961 - Sandringham, England - 7.45pm.

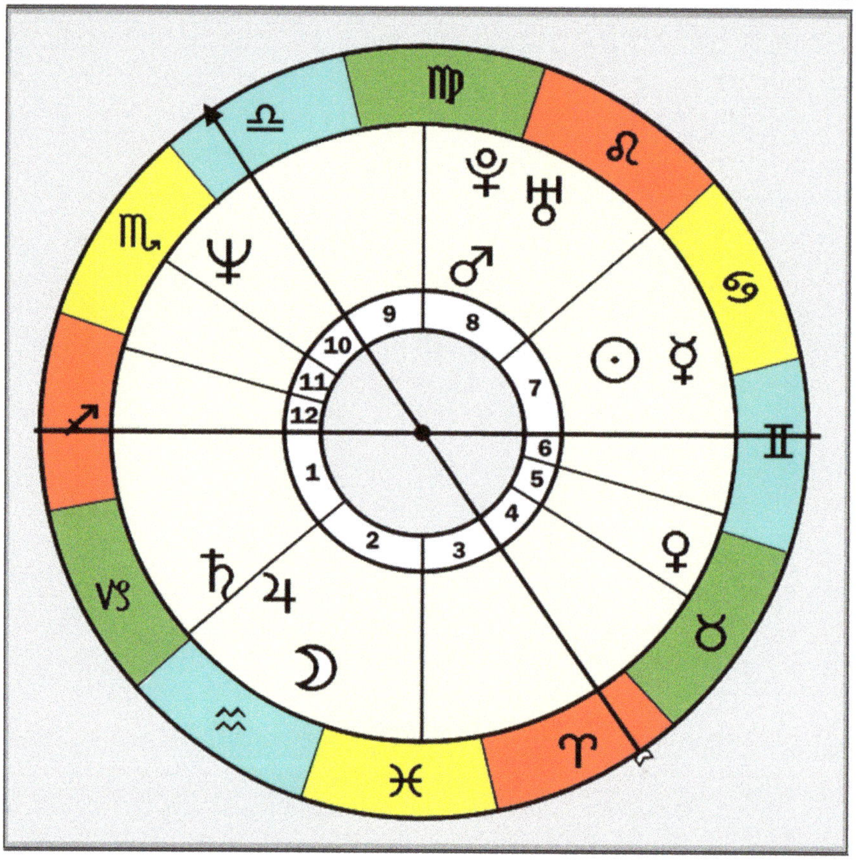

	SIGNS		PLANETS	
1	♈	Aries	♂	Mars
2	♉	Taurus	♀	Venus
3	♊	Gemini	☿	Mercury
4	♋	Cancer	☽	Moon
5	♌	Leo	☉	Sun
6	♍	Virgo	☿	Mercury

	SIGNS		PLANETS	
7	♎	Libra	♀	Venus
8	♏	Scorpio	♇	Pluto
9	♐	Sagittarius	♃	Jupiter
10	♑	Capricorn	♄	Saturn
11	♒	Aquarius	♅	Uranus
12	♓	Pisces	♆	Neptune

Figure 12 : Birth Chart of Lady Diana Spencer

PLANET POSITIONS OF THE EXAMPLE BIRTH CHART

1st. House – Self Projection (Seed) – Saturn in Capricorn (Cardinal Earth)

2nd. House – Personal Resources (Germination) – Jupiter & Moon in Aquarius (Fixed Air)

5th. House – Personal Creativity (Power. Creativity) – Venus in Taurus (Fixed Earth)

7th. House – Social Projection (Partnerships) – Sun and Mercury in Cancer (Cardinal Water)

8th. House – Social Resources – Uranus in Leo (Fixed Fire) . Mars & Pluto in Virgo (Mutable Earth)

10th. House – Social Security (Peak. Career) – Neptune in Scorpio (Fixed Water)

BIRTH CHART EXAMPLE

The lives of famous, or infamous, people are good sources for astrological analysis and study – although we cannot always know everything that goes on in the background. Here we have the additional benefit of knowing the exact time and place of birth. "The Cycle of Growth" contains a more detailed analysis.

We must not lose sight of Diana's basic Life Lesson as the main theme.

Details come from the book "Diana, Her True Story" by Andrew Morton (ISBN 1-85479-128-1)

THE MOON – THE PAST. THE MOTHER.

The Moon in a Birth Chart indicates lessons learned from the past – such as from past lives or inherited traits of character. It especially indicates the influence of our mother. Diana's mother left the family when she was 6 years of age. In those days divorce was almost unheard of as it carried a form of social stigma. As a Moon Aquarius (Fixed Air. The Mind) Diana was at "root" level an extremely independent, unconventional, individual. In the book "Diana Her True Story" we find :-

**Diana's mother ..... "was fiercely proud, combative and tough minded"*

**"She was the only girl I knew whose parents were divorced. Those things just didn't happen then."*

THE SUN – THE FUTURE. THE MAIN LIFE LESSON

With Sun in Cancer (Cardinal Water. Emotions) one's Life Lesson is based on learning to be a "mother". As this applies to males as well as females we have to extend the remit slightly. The symbol of Cancer is The Crab. The main feature of The Crab is its outer shell. Cancer people are especially emotionally sensitive, psychic even, so they need a "shell" to escape from the outside world when they need to. This is psychic self-defence. So their home is very important to them. She moved to London flat (bought by her mother) just prior to meeting Prince Charles for the second time and rented rooms to 2 friends.

***Coleherne Court ....the happiest time of her life....She always had the rubber gloves on as she clucked about the place."*

The Lesson is often based on the need to extend the "shell" to include "children" – which can mean anyone else in need of care and protection. We see that, not only was Diana fiercely protective of her own children, she also extended that to include others. Her first jobs on leaving school were as a nanny, and kindergarten teacher, and she extended this to include land mine victims and other children as patron of several related charities. Despite her general shy demeanour (Crabs normally make retreat sideways rather than directly attacking) we note that she resisted any outside control of her children by those at Buckingham Palace – such as by sacking the royal nanny, and taking William abroad against advice.

NEPTUNE

In "The Cycle of Growth" there is examination of the transit of Neptune in Diana's short lifetime which is important in her Birth Chart by being in Scorpio in her 10th. House (Career. Public view) ruled by the Sign of Libra (Partnerships) – hence the fairy tale image of "Prince and Princess". Charles is Sun Scorpio. She died at the beginning of a new Generic Jupiter Cycle (Stage 1. Seed) when transiting Neptune made a conjunction with the Saturn position in her Birth Chart. The transit covered the 1st. Octave of The Cycle of Growth which among numerous other things symbolically describes the life of Jesus from his birth to crucifixion and resurrection.

The 10th. House symbolising "Career" is opposite the 4th. House (Home. Security) which is naturally ruled by Cancer and The Moon - and we can see that her struggle to balance the two went beyond what is normal. A 10th. House Neptune (Generic or Personal) typically brings things to public view that we would rather remain hidden.

MICHAEL HUTCHENCE (1960 – 1997)

Strangely, as I completed this chapter, there was a documentary about his death on television.

Michael Hutchence was lead singer and member of a rock band INXS in Australia. He became a world famous pop icon. He was heavily involved in sex and drugs, and his name was connected with those of numerous glamorous women including Kylie Minogue. There was controversy concerning whether his death from asphyxiation was suicide, an accident, or the result of a large "cocktail" of alcohol and drugs found in his blood.

His Birth Chart is similar to Diana Spencer's by having Libra (Partnerships) on his 10th. House Cusp and Neptune in 10th. House in Scorpio. Apart from the 10th. House position, his Neptune had additional influence by being in conjunction with his Moon in Scorpio (Sex. Death).

There are similarities between his Birth Chart and Lady Diana's (remembering that they were born only 18 months apart, so the slower planets had not moved far). However, the House positions are significant considering the 24 hour rotation of the Earth.

We have the following similarities :-

1. He was a famous personality.
2. His life was constantly given media attention.
3. He had Libra (Partnerships) on the cusp of his 10th. House
4. He had Neptune in Scorpio in his 10th. House.
5. His Neptune was Sextile Pluto in Virgo in his 8th. House.
6. He died age 37 (Diana 36).
7. There was mystery concerning his death.

LIFE DIARY AND GENERIC TRANSITS EXAMPLE

We now see how the later movement of planets affected Diana's life. We start with her Life Diary and continue by seeing how it is depicted by Astrology. The actual events that occur to us as individuals depend on the Birth Chart as the main "seed" – the starting point of later growth.

- ***1. SEED. REBIRTH. Opportunity for new beginnings***
- ***4. TRANSPLANTING. Change. A step forward.***
- ***7. PARTNERSHIPS. Finding help outside one's experience and current "home base".***
- ***10. PEAK. HARVEST. Public prominence and duties. Success or failure depending on past actions. Followed by decline in preparation for a new cycle.***

Lady Diana was born in July, so the years below cover July to June.

				GENERIC HOUSES		
	Age	Year	Event	Ju	Sa	Ur
1	0	1961	* * * BIRTH. Park House, Norfolk	1	1	1
2	1	1962		2	1	1
3	2	1963		3		
4	3	1964	Brother Charles born	4		
5	4	1965		5		
6	5	1966		6		
7	6	1967	Mother moved away as a trial separation	7	4	
8	7	1968	Sent to Riddlesworth girls' boarding school	8	4	
9	8	1969	Parents' divorce	9		2
10	9	1970	Sent away to school	10		
11	10	1971		11		
12	11	1972		12		
13	12	1973	* West Heath Boarding School	1		
14	13	1974		2		
15	14	1975	Death of grandfather. Move to Althorp - family ancestral home	3		3
16	15	1976	Went to finishing school in Switzerland.	4	7	
17	16	1977	First met Prince Charles. Left school	5	7	
18	17	1978	First job as nanny. Moved to London	6		
19	18	1979		7		
20	19	1980	Met Charles at Balmoral	8		
21	20	1981	First public appearance with Charles. Married	9		
22	21	1982	Prince William born	10		4
23	22	1983	Visit Australia and Canada. Took William. Represented The Queen	11	10	
24	23	1984	Prince Harry born	12	10	
25	24	1985	Suicide attempt. Audience with the Pope. Visited AIDS victims	1		
26	25	1986	Visit British Columbia. Charles with Camilla Parker-Bowles	2		
27	26	1987	Portugal. Germany.France	3		
28	27	1988	Separation from Charles	4		
29	28	1989	Charles and Diana living apart	5		5
30	29	1990	Diana linked with James Gilbey	6		
31	30	1991	*	7	1	
32	31	1992	Father died. Official announcement of the separation	8	1	
33	32	1993		9		
34	33	1994	Leaked telephone calls made public in the press	10		
35	34	1995	Queen asked them to end marriage. Charles agreed. Diana disagree	11		
36	35	1996	Official divorce. First holiday with Dodi Al Fayed. Sold dresses.	12		6
37	36	1997	Visited Angola land mine victims. DIED	1	4	
38	37	1998		2	4	

Figure 13 : Life Diary - Lady Diana Spencer

GENERIC TRANSITS OF JUPITER AND SATURN

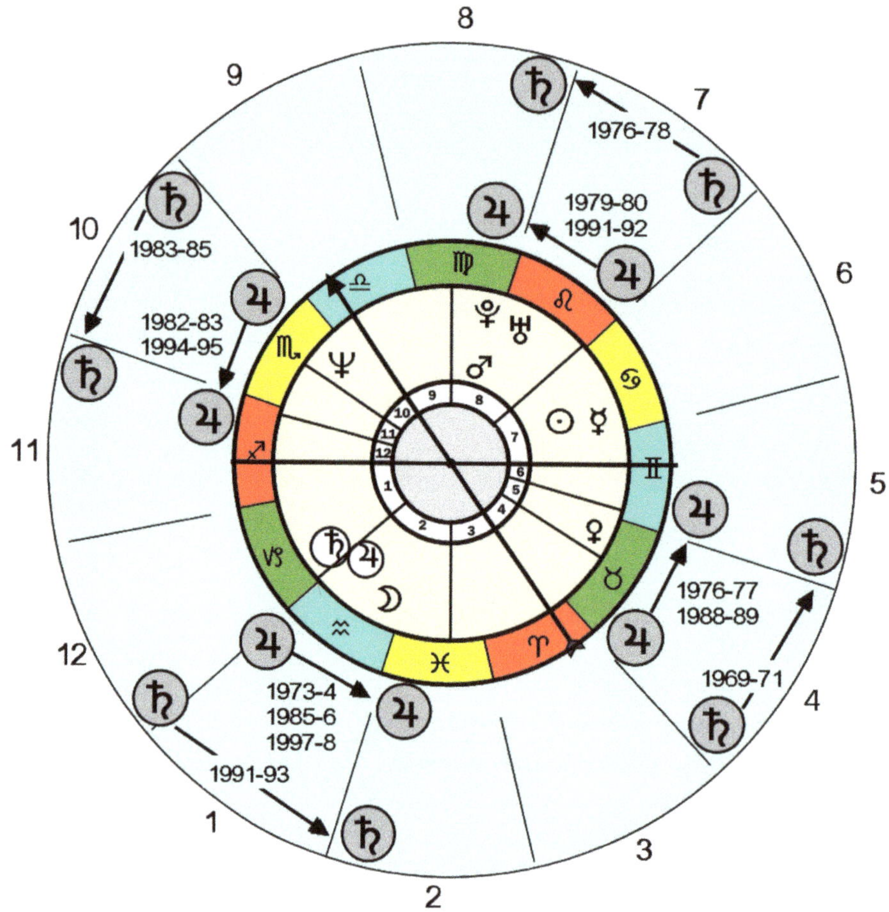

Figure 14 : Transits Chart of Lady Diana Spencer

GENERIC TRANSIT CHART DESCRIPTION

1. We see that everything is relative to the "Seed" birth as a starting point. Diana was "planted" into an aristocratic environment and rose to status of "deputy queen".
2. We emphasise that each Stage is dependent on what has gone before. If seeds are not sown and tended they wither and die.
3. The central circle shows Diana's Birth Chart with its planet positions. Outer Houses 1 to 12 (coloured blue) are the Generic Jupiter Houses. The Birth Chart positions of Jupiter and Saturn are the starting points of their Generic Cycles.
4. The outer transit circle is divided into 12 houses of 30 degrees with the cusp (beginning) of the Generic 1st.House at the birth position of Jupiter. Jupiter makes a complete cycle every 12 years. Saturn 30 years.
5. It is normal to take into account the positions of transiting planets (Personal Transits) in relationship to the Personal Houses of the Birth Chart too. I have not done so here. Diana's birth Saturn position is (just) in her Personal 1st. House so there would not be a great difference anyway. Jupiter is (just) in her Personal 2nd. House. The close proximity does not seem to affect results much. In any case, my experiments so far show that the Generic positions are better indicators of external events. The Personal ones seem to be more of an inner response to them.

6. Because Saturn is conjunct (adjoining) Jupiter in Diana's Birth Chart, we can conveniently use the same Jupiter Generic Houses for Saturn for this example.
7. The blue Transit circle shows the years when Jupiter and Saturn transited Diana's 1st., 4th., 7th., and 10th. Generic Houses. These are chosen as being at the beginning of the "quarters" - which are times of stress or conflict of energy when changes are most likely to occur (Spring, Summer, Autumn, Winter). I also include the 12th.House transits because events tend to happen at this time to clear the way for the new cycle.
8. Jupiter's 12 year transit cycle gives it approximately 1 year in each House. Jupiter's energy is broadly related to one's social standing. Its main keyword is “EXPANSION”.
9. Saturn's 30 year transit cycle gives it approximately 2 ½ years in each house. Its actions tend to oppose those of Jupiter. It's main keyword is “CONSOLIDATION”. It tends to seek practical or tangible results. Order and Structure.
10. Too much Expansion brings chaos. Too much Consolidation brings standstill.
11. Because planets appear to travel backwards through the Zodiac at times ("retrograde") the transits of planets through the Houses is very irregular. Periods of retrogradation are said to be times of "reconsideration". I have based my dates here on periods when the planet movements were Direct (forward). Their activity in a House is not ended until they finally leave it during an orbit.
12. The dates in the transit diagram are not exactly accurate in that they suggest January to December positions, whereas there could be some months difference either way. Correct dates are in the commentary where I have taken the first house entry direct and last house exit direct.
13. Diana was born in July so the Generic Houses affect July to June.
14. I have not included the first 12 year Jupiter cycle because parents have greater control of circumstances - usually until the first Saturn Return (to its birth position) around age 30 – or later at the Mid Life Crisis.
15. I have added comments about Saturn where it seems appropriate.
16. I have noticed that women often give birth during 10th. House transits by Jupiter or Saturn. Here we see both.
17. You will note that we use the same keywords for a House transit no matter what planet we are referring to, or whether the transit is Personal or Generic. The difference is the activity of the planet under consideration. They are similar, but not identical, to those used for the Birth Chart houses, which refer to internal, personal, individual factors rather than external ones. The Birth Chart refers more to one's natural, instinctive, reactions to external circumstances until one gains more self-discipline and development of Will. Any Birth Chart trait of character or personality, can be changed by use of Will, as can the outcome of events. Acting from decisions based on objective here-and-now data processing rather than gut reaction (unless one has learned to trust it) or hearsay.
18. Diana died at age 36 which is the beginning of a new 12 year Jupiter cycle - Cycle of Growth Stage 1 (Seed). Neptune was making a PERSONAL 1st.House transit at the same time (Seed). We can see that she was beginning to make a new life for herself.
19. Any planets placed in the main Personal houses at the 4 quarters of a Birth Chart (Houses 1,4,7,10) have a greater influence than others. Diana's chart has Neptune in the 10th. House of Career.
20. I have not made any judgements here. I have merely recorded the relationship between transits and events. If any judgements were to be made it would have been for Diana to do so.

COMPARISON OF TRANSITS AND LIFE EVENTS

We look at the crisis stages of Jupiter and add notes about Saturn where appropriate.

1973 – Age 12 - Cycle of Growth Stage 1 (Seed. Aries. Mars)

We begin here because earlier in life we are more under the control of our parents. As is common in Britain a major step forward comes when we enter secondary school. One of Jupiter's rulerships is over schools and other places of more academic than practical learning by personal experience – such as from books.

1976 – Age 15 – Cycle of Growth Stage 4 (Transplanting. Cancer. Moon)

Diana went to finishing school in Switzerland.

Saturn was at Cycle of Growth Stage 7 (Partnerships) at that time when she met Prince Charles for the first time – although he was dating her older sister, and she was "too young to date". He was 10 years older.

1979 – Age 18 – Cycle of Growth Stage 7 (Partnerships. Libra. Venus)

A focus of this Stage is that we leave the home to enter a more public domain. Diana moved to London and began working. We could consider her mother as her "partner" in the enterprise because she bought the flat for Diana. Her job as nanny reflects her Cancer Sun Sign ("The Mother")

The following year she met Charles once again at Balmoral and began their relationship. They were married in 1981.

1982 – Age 21 – Cycle of Growth Stage 10 (Peak. Harvest. Capricorn. Saturn)

This Stage is the culmination of a cycle where the results come to public view for good or ill. This is followed by a decline in activity in preparation for the beginning of the new cycle later on.

We have the first official public appearance with Charles and the birth of Prince William. I have noticed in my research that women often give birth during a 10th. House transit. Cycle of Growth Stage 10 includes the symbolism of Capricorn and the Christmas Story of the birth of Jesus THE SON, and the rebirth of THE SUN at the Winter Equinox.

Saturn was also at its own Cycle of Growth Stage 10 for 2 years after that, which adds additional emphasis. In this case Diana made official visits with Charles to Australia and Canada. She actually represented The Queen at the funeral of Princess Grace of Monaco.

1984 - Cycle of Growth Stage 12 (Withdrawal. Confinement. Pisces. Jupiter or Neptune)

Prince Harry was born in 1984.

The Stage is symbolic of the time of Confinement before birth when we see the activity of 12th House "clearing the past" in preparation for a new cycle. Receiving "punishment" or rewards for past efforts (Karma). There is a tendency for events to occur now, rather than at the next stage. Diana received some honorary titles and she and Charles had an audience with The Pope.

She had a publicised suicide attempt – although later she admitted to "2 or 3". The old Diana was due to "die".

1985 – Age 24 – Cycle of Growth Stage 1 (Seed. Aries. Mars)

Typically for the Stage, there was not much happening on the surface at this time. Diana continued formal visits with Charles although they were beginning to separate in private as he became more involved with Camilla Parker-Bowles. However, we can see that she was now beginning to find her feet on a more personal path.

She upset The Palace by publicly becoming involved with AIDS and leprosy victims.

The OFFICIAL (Saturn) announcement of the separation does not occur until Saturn's Cycle of Growth Stage 1 in 1992.

The actual divorce does not occur until Jupiter's next Cycle of Growth Stage 1.

1988- Age 27 – Cycle of Growth Stage 4 (Transplanting. Cancer. Moon)

The Transplanting in this case was Diana and Charles starting to live apart. Diana moved away.

1991 – Age 30 – Cycle of Growth Stage 7 (Partners. Libra. Venus)

Although there were other suggested relationships, Diana was publicly linked with James Gilbey.

Saturn (Tradition. The Establishment. Father) was beginning a new Cycle of Growth Stage 1 (Seed). Symbolically this is the time when one has been following the life pattern defined by one's parents until now, and there is opportunity to find a more personal pathway based on one's own life experience. We first note that in the not too distant past not many people lived much beyond this age. Secondly, this is the time of life when we begin to deteriorate physically. For example, men in sport are no longer able to compete with younger people, and women are facing menopause.

This would have been especially traumatic for Diana because she was brought up in the strict traditions (Saturn/Capricorn) of British aristocracy.

At this time Diana lost 2 "father figures". Her father died, and her separation from Charles (10 years her senior) was announced OFFICIALLY (which again refers to Saturn/Capricorn. They had been living apart for some time beforehand).

1994 – Age 33 – Cycle of Growth Stage 10 (Peak. Harvest. Capricorn. Saturn)

Once again Diana's achievements of the Cycle come to public view. The Partnership with James Gilbey came to the public eye in the form of telephone calls leaked to the press. This is followed by a decline in activity in preparation for the beginning of the new cycle later on. In fact, she eventually reduced the number of charities she supported to just 6.

In 1995 we have an example of Cycle of Growth Stage 11 (Discontent. Aquarius. Saturn or Uranus) where the Uranus call is to make one's individual stand against repressive Saturn demands. The Queen wrote letters to Diana and Charles asking them to formally end their marriage. Charles agreed, but Diana refused – wanting time to consider. We note a similarity with the earlier time of separation when the official, formal, announcement came some time after the event.

1996 - Cycle of Growth Stage 12 (Withdrawal. Confinement. Pisces. Jupiter or Neptune)

As in 1984 we have preparation for the beginning of a new cycle. Diana agreed to the divorce and negotiated a favourable settlement. The divorce was announced officially. She had her first holiday with Dodi El Fayed.

We note the Stage 12 connection with (rumoured) use of alcohol and drugs.

1997 – Age 36 – Cycle of Growth Stage 1 (Seed. Aries. Mars)

We now arrive at the year of Diana's death in a car crash. We see that she was beginning to make a new life for herself distinct from her previous "official" role as Princess of Wales. She reduced her involvement (royal patronage. Saturn) with over 100 charities to just 6. During this year she sold many of her old dresses in New York and gave the proceeds to charity. We can see this as a symbol of her "new appearance". She visited Angola dressed in an army flak jacket and gave support to the International Campaign to Ban Landmines and The Red Cross. It is suggested that this finally got the international Ottawa Treaty to ban land mines agreed.

We have to note :-

1. The beginning of the previous Cycle was preceded by her suicide attempts.
2. She died in a tunnel – symbolic of Transition and Change.
3. Neptune has a powerful position in her Birth Chart. Following her death there were conspiracy theories and suggestions of involvement with alcohol and drugs - which have connections with Neptune/Pisces. One of the functions of Neptune is to blur or confuse ("dissolve") practical and emotional matters to clear the way for Change. Neptune includes "glamour" that can disguise reality.

<u>Saturn was also at its own Generic Cycle of Growth Stage 4 (Transplanting)</u>

This gave an additional pressure for Crisis and Change.

In "The Cycle of Growth" I show that this Stage is associated with the Tarot Card "The Chariot" – which, in modern terms, can be considered as a motor car. The historical chariot and motor car can be considered to be much more than a form of travel – among other things, it is a symbol of status. There is additional relationship with the Sign of Cancer – as the "shell" of The Crab as a form of defence, and the psychological Persona - or "mask" of the actor concealing his true identity to play a part on the Stage of Life.

Figure 15 : Tarot Card VII - The Chariot

THE CYCLE OF GROWTH

This chapter refers to the contents of my 496 page book "The Cycle of Growth" published in 2015. The 8 ½ x 11 size is necessary because the book contains numerous drawings and diagrams – many full page in colour – which is necessary in view of the large amount of detail they contain. The concept of "Your Personal Life Diary" is included and expanded.

FREE PDF A4 ARTWORK SAMPLES DOWNLOAD

- **"The Cycle of Growth Picture Book"** containing all the artwork, and PDF and Excel versions of "The Life Diary" form are available by using this link :-
  www.CycleOfGrowth.com
- By leaving your email address you will also be given the opportunity of a limited special offer when "The Cycle of Growth" is published.

OVERVIEW

The main principle of The Cycle of Growth is that all cyclic processes, no matter how many stages we split them into, are manifestations of the same Whole. In each cycle the positive and negative forces balance one another to return to the original Zero State. When we compare the Cycle of Growth with seeming different areas of study there is remarkable correspondence.

The book compares traditional philosophic and esoteric teachings with some of the latest discoveries in Psychology and Science - the most important being the discovery of the Transcendent Planets Uranus, Neptune, and Pluto, the now accepted story of Evolution beginning with The Big Bang , and the modern scientific use of Number Zero - which was not recognised in earlier history. We also consider insights given by the trance medium Edgar Cayce - who also gave verifiable information about people he never met. This also reconciles differences when authorities on a subject disagree.

This book therefore contains concepts not found elsewhere, and assumes no prior knowledge of the subjects it contains.

ASTROLOGY AND PSYCHOLOGY

- Ancient philosophy did not include knowledge of the psychological concepts that are available to everyone today, although it was present in symbolic form. We also recognise that , as with the Hunter Gatherer, the mental psychology was different to that of today because the Jungian Thinking Function has developed from the general public access to Reading, Writing, and Mathematics - which are also relatively new subjects.
- It is becoming recognised that our experiences in the womb affect our later life. When we compare the Astrological Logarithmic Timescale of a human lifetime from Conception to Death with The "Development of Personality" stages of Freud, Erikson, and Piaget there is exact correspondence.
- The Logarithmic Timescale also adds a "Transcendent Octave" which gives rise to evolutionary development.
- The planet Uranus clearly relates to the Jungian psychological concept of The Individuation Process.
- Now in The Age of Aquarius, we can use recent historical discoveries to understand the other Zodiac Ages.

THE TAROT

- The 22 symbols of the Major Arcana match the 12 Cycle of Growth Stages in sequence.

NUMEROLOGY

- Traditional philosophical systems and Numerology do not include Number Zero because it is a relatively new discovery – only becoming a number in its own right in the Computer Age.
- The sequence of Numbers corresponds with the process of Evolution – and therefore The Cycle of Growth - from The Big Bang onwards, as demonstrated by the development of all Chemical Elements from basic Hydrogen.

THE KABBALAH TREE OF LIFE

- This symbolic system gets closer to the archetypal universal principles than the others and therefore associates with all other areas of study to the enrichment of them all.
- The Astrological symbol of Neptune is a basic depiction of the 3 Pillars of The Tree of Life.
- With the discovery of Number Zero, we are now able to associate Numbers Zero to 9 with the 10 Sephiroth of The Tree – which was not previously possible.

- With the discovery of the Transcendent Planets we are able to add them to The Tree of Life where there were traditionally no planetary associations.
- "The Lightning Flash" of Kabbalist involution and related Astrological planets exactly matches those of the sequence of stages in The Cycle of Growth. We can now add a Transcendent function to The Tree which was not apparent before.

THE BIBLE

- The Life of Jesus and the Genesis Story of Creation relate to our life in the womb and The Transcendent Octave of The Cycle of Growth.
- The first 3 chapters of Genesis relate to the scientific "Big Bang Theory" and the 3 Octaves of The Cycle of Growth.
- The Tree of Life mentioned in Genesis and Revelation (and The Kabbalah) refers to the human Chakra System of energy centres in the human body, and the related hormone-producing endocrine glands.

A SUMMARY TABLE FOLLOWS

It includes correspondences between :

1. The Cycle of Growth Stages Meanings
2. Astrology : Houses
3. Astrology : Zodiac Signs
4. Astrology : Planets
5. Numbers (Numerology)
6. The Tarot

Figure 16 : The Cycle of Growth Summary Table

INDEX

www.ingramcontent.com/pod-product-compliance
Ingram Content Group UK Ltd.
Pitfield, Milton Keynes, MK11 3LW, UK
UKHW062001290726
14090UKWH00021B/1326

9 780993 092619